Double Dutch

Architecture in the Netherlands Since 1985

Bernard Hulsman text
Luuk Kramer photos

nai010 publishers

Foreword

As the 1980s drew to a close, a breeze of enlightenment blew through the world of Dutch architecture. Postmodernism was on the way out having left the Netherlands reasonably unscathed, as Wouter Deen, Christoph Grafe and Bernard Leupen observed in 1990 in their introduction to the Dutch-language compilation whose title translates as 'How modern is Dutch architecture?' 'Like others before it this dangerous storm passed by the country behind the dykes', according to the three professors at the Faculty of Architecture at Delft University of Technology. Dutch architects had shown little interest in the fashionable caprices of postmodernism. 'So the continuity with the heroic Modern Movement of the 1920s remained unbroken.'

But the Dutch architects and critics were too soon in breathing a collective sigh of relief. Five years later postmodernism arrived after all with the completion of Adolfo Natalini's redevelopment of Waagstraat in Groningen. Hot on the heels of this breakthrough came a tidal wave of neo-traditional architecture that saw the Luxembourg postmodernist Rob Krier emerge as the most influential architect in the Netherlands.

The professional press paid scant attention to postmodern architecture in the Netherlands. Most concern was for what would become known as SuperDutch architecture, after a book by Bart Lootsma published in 2000. Many critics felt that a new kind of 'conceptual' architecture had arrived in the Netherlands in the wake of Rem Koolhaas's OMA, an architecture that was perfectly in tune with the age of digitization and globalization. This gave the Netherlands an international reputation around the year 2000 of 'most modern architecture country in the world'. Anyone seeking to spoil the party by pointing out that postmodernism had finally broken through in this country, and how, was told they were flogging a dead horse. After all it was common knowledge that by the turn of the millennium postmodernism was long dead and buried.

But the fact that postmodernism is not dead even now can be borne out by two logical arguments. First, in the 1980s Rob Krier was a prominent advocate of postmodernism. Thirty years later his ideas are still the same. This means that Krier is still a postmodernist. Second, Rob Krier was one of the most successful architects in the Netherlands in recent years. Not only that, his formula for success has been widely adopted. As a result postmodernism blossomed in this country in the years before and after the turn of the millennium.

Double Dutch tells for the first time the whole story of the golden years of Dutch architecture, from 1985 to 2010. It describes not just the rise of the conceptual SuperDutch architecture but also that of postmodernism, Wilde Wonen (literally: Wild Living), Islamic architecture and 'sustainability'.

The common thread in this story is the belief among architects and critics in the Zeitgeist, a belief that refuses to go away entirely. Since the beginning of the nineteenth century the key *raison d'être* of new architectural styles has been that they rhyme with the spirit of the age. Older styles competing with them are branded passé and anachronistic.

That said, *Double Dutch* shows that in the golden quarter century of Dutch architecture the Zeitgeist was not speaking plain language. Thus twenty years ago we saw Deconstructivists and computer architects alike invoking the spirit of the time to justify their architecture, yet their styles could not have been more different. And although Wilde Wonen, the proposal for a deregulated housing construction market, fitted perfectly with the neoliberal Zeitgeist then prevailing, it still failed to take off in the years before and after 2000. It was postmodernism, the very movement that had been declared dead, that proved to work wonderfully well in Dutch housing, which by then had been liberalized.

If the Zeitgeist had anything to say in the past decades, it was unintelligible. Call it 'double Dutch'.

De Meander Amsterdam

Rob Krier 2001

As the twenty-first century began, the Luxembourg architect Rob Krier was the most influential architect in the Netherlands with housing schemes like De Meander in Amsterdam. His urban design, as exemplified by Brandevoort, a 'Vinex' housing development in Helmond, has been particularly influential. Vinex is a Dutch acronym for 'Supplement to the Fourth National Policy Document on Physical Planning' (Vierde Nota Ruimtelijke Ordening Extra). 'The Dutch have a penchant for romanticism – that's the only reason I can think of', said Krier in 2003 as an explanation of his success in this country. 'The great thing about the Netherlands is that there's room for traditional architecture alongside the hypermodern architecture of Koolhaas and the like. I'm not the only one to enjoy success with traditional work. Brandevoort, for example, consists almost entirely of work by Dutch architects. In this respect the Netherlands is a very tolerant country. I've discovered that it's very difficult to be tolerant. In Germany they regard me as some kind of fascist. Germans are still very pre-occupied with their Nazi past and that still dictates the architectural discourse. Any call for traditional architecture is treated with suspicion in Germany because the Nazis were in favour of it.'

Eyes that Do Not See

Introduction

What's cooler than cool? SuperDutch!

In the Netherlands even suburbia, ordinarily a haven of middle-classness and banality, is cool, according to the American journalist Christopher Hawthorne in a 2004 article about Vinex developments in *The New York Times*. So much spectacular architecture could be found in among the normal houses in the new Dutch suburbs then being built that the article opened with the words 'Leave it to the Dutch to make suburbia cool.'

Hawthorne was not the first foreign journalist to visit the Netherlands to view the phenomenon of the new Dutch architecture. He was preceded by a regiment of architecture critics from Europe, Japan and America whose praises gave the Netherlands the reputation of being the most modern architecture country in the world. Here, in this little country on the North Sea, the future of architecture was on show, as many critics and architects would claim in the years around 2000.

The foreign journalists were here mainly to see the work of architects whom the critic Bart Lootsma had dubbed SuperDutch in the year 2000. On the face of it, the SuperDutch brigade, amongst whom Neutelings Riedijk Architects, Lars Spuybroek, Ben van Berkel and of course Rem Koolhaas, are a motley crew. And yet they largely shared the same position on architecture, which can be best described by the term 'conceptual'. 'Form follows concept' is their slogan: many SuperDutch architects distil from the client's brief a high-powered idea, a 'concept', that lends direction to the design as a whole.

It is no coincidence that the careers of a number of SuperDutch architects, including Winy Maas of MVRDV and Willem Jan Neutelings of Neutelings Riedijk, began at Rem Koolhaas's Office for Metropolitan Architecture (OMA). Koolhaas's influence on the SuperDutch phenomenon and on Dutch architecture in general is impossible to overestimate. His scenario-like approach to architecture and urbanism, with 'what if?' asked at every turn, was a first step towards 'conceptual' architecture. OMA's pioneering work likewise resonates in, for example, MVRDV's datascapes, the all but outdated functionalist design method in which a welter of statistical data points the design in a particular direction.

Back in 1980 or thereabouts, Koolhaas had shown with his early work, such as the IJplein residential area in Amsterdam, how to reuse the 'heroic modernism' of the interwar years. A devotee of Ivan Leonidov and the Russian Constructivists, he and others teaching at the Faculty of Architecture at Delft University of Technology were responsible for 'schoolteachers' modernism', a trend that was particularly popular among young architects around 1990.

A second reason often given for the ascendancy of Dutch architecture in the years 1985 to 2010 besides Koolhaas was the support given to architects by the government. Since the time of the French occupation in the early 1800s, the Netherlands has had a Government Architect who advises the government on matters of architecture. In the 1980s and 1990s, an architectural infrastructure was assembled that was unlike anything anywhere before or since. To begin with, 1991 saw the publication of the first in a series of white papers on architecture in which the national government formulated its architecture policy. Large municipalities followed suit with their own 'architecture memoranda', often resulting in the establishment of architecture centres, of which the country now has more than 30. In 1993 the Netherlands Architecture Fund was set up, its most important task being to subsidize architecture in the broadest sense of the word. In that same year the Netherlands Architecture Institute (NAI), which had been founded in 1988, moved to a new building in Rotterdam designed by Jo Coenen. With the NAI's inception in 1988 came the first of the *Architecture in the Netherlands Yearbooks*, which burgeoned into an institution in its own right. It was brought out by NAI Publishers, which together with other publishers specialized in architecture such as 010 Publishers and SUN Architecture, provided a steady flow of Dutch and English books on the subject. The Berlage Institute, a postgraduate institution to promote 'excellence in architecture and urban design', was founded in 1990. And since 2001 Rotterdam has hosted an International Architecture Biennale (IABR).

It is impossible to measure with any accuracy the extent to which that infrastructure helped Dutch architecture to flourish in the period between 1985 and 2010. But it is an undisputed fact that many young architects took the first steps in their career with, say, a start-up grant from the Netherlands Foundation for Visual Arts, Design and Architecture (Fonds BKVB). Experimental architecture and books by old, large architectural practices were also eligible for subsidies. Thus, for example, as late as 1999 Rem Koolhaas was awarded a subsidy of almost 14,000 euros by Fonds BKVB to take part in a competition to design an arts centre in Rome. The NAI mounted with some regularity travelling exhibitions featuring the work of young Dutch talent that most certainly helped to promote Dutch architecture in other countries.

The development of a comprehensive Dutch infrastructure for architecture was largely the result of dissatisfaction among architects and administrators of cities and housing corporations about the shabby architecture being produced in the early 1980s. Urban renewal, then in full swing, bore the main brunt of such criticism. Here quantity came before quality, not least because the economic crisis at the end of the 1970s had hit the Dutch housing market hard.

Administrators and architects then embarked on various enterprises to reinstate architecture as a 'cultural brief'. In The Hague, alderman Adri Duivesteijn, who would later be the first director of the NAI, showed how the quality of urban renewal architecture could be improved. He deployed not only renowned foreign architects like the Belgian Charles Vandenhove and the Portuguese Alvaro Siza but also young Dutch architects such as the four members of Mecanoo. In 1987 Duivesteijn was one of the initiators of 5 x 5, a task force in which administrators and architects had joined forces. The group sought to draw attention to the importance of good architecture with debates and the booklet *Voorbij het gangbare* (Beyond current practice). And they succeeded. The Netherlands of the 1990s was awash with councillors and other officials handing out commissions to architects of repute, not infrequently resorting to the *Architecture Yearbook* for their choice.

Soon after 1985, the Netherlands became a country of extraordinary architecture. Housing corporations, which had always been convinced that a workers' dwelling had to offer more than just shelter and should serve as a 'cultural' brief, were especially prepared to take risks. Mecanoo, Liesbeth van der Pol and Marlies Rohmer are just three of the many architects to get their first commissions from a housing corporation; indeed, the designers comprising Mecanoo still had to graduate from university.

That many young architects landed large commissions early on in their career had a lot do with the new major building projects facing this country in the 1990s. After urban renewal, the biggest building project of the previous two decades, came the Vinex developments, the new generation of suburbs where some 750,000 housing units were to be built. The 'urban restructuring' of the post-war residential areas began at the same time. Add to these the restructuring of old abandoned industrial and dockland areas as new city districts, such as Kop van Zuid in Rotterdam and the eastern docks area

(Oostelijk Havengebied) in Amsterdam. The country's infrastructure also proved ripe for repairing and extending: dikes had to be strengthened, bridges heightened, motorways widened or run through tunnels and new ones constructed. Schiphol, the country's national airport, required constant expansion and grew, largely to designs by Benthem Crouwel Architekten, into a full-scale work city. And although work on the high-speed rail system (HSL) proceeded at a glacial pace in the Netherlands, it did give rise to new traffic nodes in Arnhem, Rotterdam and elsewhere.

Often, the construction of the new traffic nodes was an inducement to redevelop the areas around the old railways stations. Thus, Arnhem gained two office towers designed by Ben van Berkel alongside his still-to-be-completed HSL station; and today in Utrecht and Rotterdam the area around the redeveloped stations are getting an overhaul. Even cities not earmarked for new traffic nodes, such as Maastricht, Enschede, Almere, Zaandam and Spijkenisse, have modernized their centres. The steady economic growth in the Netherlands in the years 1985–2008 also saw the construction of an immense number of business parks and countless office buildings.

Remarkably, the renovation and redesign of the Netherlands was accompanied by a revolution, or perhaps more accurately a counter-revolution, in Dutch architecture, one that eluded most national and international critics and journalists for quite a while. They had, to borrow Le Corbusier's description, 'eyes that did not see'. Most did make a connection between the modernizing of the Netherlands and the rise of architecture by SuperDutch offices, but the belated spectacular breakthrough of postmodernism passed them by.

The most important reason for their blindness was that the Netherlands was a country where the modernist tradition had seemed unbroken until deep into the 1990s: many young architects who had begun their careers a decade earlier were disciples of neo- or schoolteachers' modernism. Yet as their careers took flight during the 1990s, postmodernism made its belated entry into the Netherlands. Just before the turn of the millennium, mainly in the shape of neo-traditionalism, it would take on tidal wave proportions.

Purper Project Delft

Molenaar & Co architecten 2010

Joris Molenaar, who from 1985 to 2009 co-ran an office with Wilfried van Winden, is one of the few Dutch architects who was not averse to traditionalism in the 1980s. 'We're quite happy to accommodate the past', Joris Molenaar said in 2001 of his work. 'But we're not traditionalists the way Kropholler was. For Kropholler traditionalism was bound up with a perception of mankind and with Catholicism. That's not an issue anymore.' Molenaar's restructuring of Purper, a block of flats dating from the 1960s, sees many developments in Dutch architecture of the past 25 years converge. The project is part of the urban restructuring of Poptahof, a modernist area of Delft. By adding a row of single-family houses and a five-storey apartment block to the original building, this part of Poptahof takes on a greater element of enclosure. Not just that, traditionalist elements were added to the stern modernist forms of the original Purper building. The brick facade has been enlivened with ceramic decorations by Christine Jette.

Civic Centre Heerlen

Jo Coenen 1985

This civic centre on Raadhuisplein in Heerlen, which Coenen designed with Piet Mertens, marked the start of his illustrious career. Like this building, a response to Frits Peutz's classical-modern masterwork of 1942 on the same square, Coenen's other early designs bore classical features. Critics regarded them as signifying a resurgence of architecture as a 'cultural brief'.
Over the years, that element of classicism disappeared from Coenen's architecture. But his urban design remained resolutely classicist. The introverted monumental blocks of housing on KNSM-eiland in Amsterdam and the *Céramique* site in Maastricht, both masterplanned by Coenen, were a reversion to the pre-modern urbanism of the likes of Berlage's Amsterdam Zuid.

The Lean Years

Chapter 1

Just how lean the early 1980s were for Dutch architecture is readily apparent at Raadhuisplein, the town hall square, in Heerlen. On it stands the civic centre, a building that originally housed a library, a chamber of commerce and the municipal museum. Completed in 1985, it was then generally regarded as the onset of a beautiful future for Dutch architecture, which had been in dire straits since around the turn of the decade.

Yet looking at this building designed by the then young Jo Coenen (b. 1949) more than a quarter century later one is struck by its shabbiness. Pessimists might see it as bearing out the assertion that architecture does not progress. Indeed, in this case it could be said to regress: the library is utterly outclassed by the town hall of 1942 diagonally across the square. Coenen's building was a response to this wartime masterpiece by Frits Peutz (1896–1974). Like the town hall it is a synthesis of classicism and modernism, but every comparison is to the disadvantage of the civic centre. Its forms are much more roughly hewn: anything as subtle as the jutting crown of the town hall's front facade is sadly lacking. Even the finish is ungainly. If the town hall is stone clad, the frontage of the civic centre sports the pale brick and plastic cladding panels disfiguring so much Dutch architecture of the 1980s.

Another building that reveals the threadbare state of early 1980s architecture is the young people's social housing on Kruisplein in Rotterdam from that same year of 1985. This pioneering example of schoolteachers' modernism, the first commission landed by the four then very youthful architects of Mecanoo, was likewise seen at the time as proof that Dutch architecture was on the mend. And here too we today are struck by its shabbiness: like so many buildings of that decade the young people's housing has not aged well.

Even the work of older, established architects in the first half of the 1980s has a skimpiness about it. The neo-rationalist work of Wim Quist, Carel Weeber and Jan Hoogstad, a reaction to the 'cosy' architecture of the 1970s, was not only matter-of-fact and anonymous but also intractable in its predominance of geometric planes and even downright boring at times. The crowning achievement of neo-rationalism was Weeber's De Zwarte Madonna in The Hague, once again from 1985, a housing block near Centraal Station whose exterior was clad from top to bottom with black tiles. Was clad, as the 'Black Madonna' has already been demolished.

Housing from the early 1980s was particularly prone to sliding from threadbare into positively down-at-heel. Many architects wrestled with the legacy of the 'critical seventies', when domestic architecture found itself in thrall to 'cosiness' and the small-scale. These goals were often achieved by resorting to a watered-down structuralism in both architecture and planning, resulting in what are now disparagingly described as 'cauliflower resorts' – residential enclaves of undefined areas of street surrounded by houses bristling with appurtenances and recesses.

This structuralist legacy was joined by a major housing crisis in the wake of the oil crises of the 1970s. House prices plummeted, partly since mortgage interest rates had risen to an unprecedented level of 12 per cent. Housing production dropped as well, to a little less than 80,000 housing units in 1979. Seven years earlier this had been 155,000 units, still the absolute record for Dutch housing production.

Central government responded with a classic Keynesian strategy: to prevent the collapse of the building construction industry, one of this country's key industries, it sought to stimulate the new build of rented units with subsidies for, among other things, urban renewal projects and houses for one- and two-person households. And it worked: at the onset of the 1980s the housing sector held up reasonably well, despite the falling house prices, with an annual production of some 100,000 units. But this came at a price. At the start of the 1980s budgets for domestic construction were at an all-time low, the upshot being new residential developments full of poor-quality housing units.

Stylistically, the most remarkable hallmark of Dutch architecture of those years was the ultra-timid presence of postmodernism. While postmodernism had triumphed at the Venice Architecture Biennale in 1980 and had dominated the International Building Exhibition in West Berlin in and around that year, in the Netherlands it remained confined to cautious attempts by young architects like Jo Coenen and Sjoerd Soeters to reconcile classicism with modernism. An extravagant postmodernism with explicit quotes from architectural history, as exemplified by Ricardo Bofill's vast housing developments in the Parisian suburbs, gave this country a miss.

The main reason postmodernism was held at arm's length in the Dutch architectural world came in the shape of Aldo van Eyck (1918–1999), the spiritual father of structuralism and 'the conscience of post-war Dutch architecture'. Proceeding principally from the fact that big buildings take on 'human' proportions by being assembled from small units, structuralism was a critique of post-war functionalism, which in Van Eyck's eyes had produced suburbs that were monotonous and technocratic.

Van Eyck's body of built work, the most famous of which would be the orphanage in Amsterdam (1960), is smaller than that of his former comrade-in-arms Herman Hertzberger. But as one of the prime movers in the Team 10 group of international architects, Van Eyck wielded greater power. He was a spider in the web of architecture. He taught at the Amsterdam Academy of Architecture and with *Forum* magazine under his co-editorship from 1959 to 1963 it became the mouthpiece for 'another idea', that of structuralism. Later, from 1966 to 1976, he was professor at what was then Delft Polytechnic, sat on numerous competition panels and advisory committees and engaged in the architectural discourse with many lectures and articles.

As a critical reaction to modernism, Van Eyck's structuralism is essentially postmodern. This explains the inclusion of work by him in *The Language of Post-Modern Architecture*, the book in which the British-American architecture critic Charles Jencks introduced the concept of postmodernism in architecture in 1977. But Van Eyck himself was unwilling to go through life as a postmodernist. Indeed, around 1980 postmodernism was the key target of Van Eyck's polemic lectures and articles. A classic example is 'Rats, Posts and Other Pests (RPP)', the lecture he gave at the Royal Institute of British Architects in London in 1981. The title says it all: this is a rabid tirade against rationalism and postmodernism. In this marvellously incoherent lecture Van Eyck makes the connection between postmodernism and crime. The postmodern architect Robert Venturi he designates as Robert V., adding as an explanation to his British listeners that in the Netherlands the names of lawbreakers are abbreviated in the press. He also draws a comparison several times between postmodernism and fascism – something that still happens today in this country. It only takes a few paragraphs of 'RPP' before Hitler's chief architect Albert Speer gets a mention. A little later Van Eyck claims that postmodernism is in the process of becoming proto- or intellectual fascism. He also accuses postmodernists of antihumanism and pornography. Postmodernists are, in short, fascist perverts, rats and pests and, as listeners and readers were expected to assume, should be eradicated.

Van Eyck's most quoted criticism levelled at the postmodernists in 'RPP' is that of 'betrayal'. What exactly they had betrayed remains unclear, but presumably this was betrayal of the cause. And the cause, as Van Eyck was at great pains to point out, was the work of the Great Gang, his collective name for the pioneers of modernism. Its members included artists like Picasso and Mondrian, relativity theorist Albert Einstein – Van Eyck was besotted with physics as a means of legitimizing his architecture – and architects like the Dutchman Johannes Duiker. Their work represented 'good', humanist modernism and the postmodernists were betraying this with their return to traditionalism, classicism, eclecticism and other historical styles of architecture.

According to Van Eyck the postmodernists had failed to understand the modern age. What the Great Gang had achieved, he felt, was still of great value in 1981. So the 'RPP' lecture was in essence the simple assertion that postmodernism was anachronistic.

Like so many architects, Van Eyck was a great believer in Zeitgeist. This belief has deep roots as revealed by the British architectural historian David Watkin in 1977. It is grounded in a German romantic idea found in the early nineteenth-century idealist philosophy of Hegel and other German thinkers, as Watkin shows in his book *Morality and Architecture*. Hegel and his Marxist heirs believed that the history of mankind was progressing towards a specific goal. Those with a knowledge of this goal - such as Karl Marx, who later in the nineteenth-century was convinced that capitalism would inevitably lead first to socialism and eventually to communism - were aware of what is advantageous, or detrimental, to achieving that goal. This created a profound moral issue: whoever brought that historical goal closer was acting in accordance with the spirit of the age and was morally correct, whereas whoever obstructed or opposed the way forward was against progress and therefore anachronistic and immoral.

For architectural historians like Nikolaus Pevsner (1902–1983) and Sigfried Giedion (1888–1968), the authors of *Pioneers of Modern Design* (1936) and *Space, Time and Architecture* (1941) respectively, architectural histories that are still read today, the International Style of the interwar years, what would later be called modernism, was the architectural equivalent of Marx's socialism. Just as capitalism would inevitably lead to socialism, so the International Style was the crowning achievement of architectural history. Architects who continued to work along traditional lines were reactionaries who denied the way forward.

At the start of the twenty-first century there was not a single architect or historian who still believed that modernism was the highest stage in the history of architecture. That said, belief in the spirit of the times is as strong as ever. To this day, the most used legitimation of a new style is that it is in keeping with the Zeitgeist; by contrast, the worst accusation you can level at an architect is that of being anachronistic. Which is why postmodernism and neo-traditionalism continue to incite moral indignation among Dutch architects and critics. And like Van Eyck some still tend to make a connection between neo-traditionalism and populism or, worse still, fascism.

Postmodernism is itself a hopelessly confusing notion. Like Aldo van Eyck, the Deconstructivist architects of the 1990s such as Peter Eisenman were adamant that their work was *not* to be labelled postmodern, even though they drew on out-and-out postmodern philosophers such as Gilles Deleuze and Jacques Derrida to lend credence to their topsy-turvy buildings. And even if the young Dutch neo-modernists often quoted from the Modern Architecture of between the wars, they felt in no way related to postmodernists, who did the same thing with older architecture.

Postmodernism may be vague as a catch-all term but there can be no misunderstanding about its essence. It was a response to the spartan, technocratic architecture and urban planning that modernism had become in the 1950s and 1960s. Postmodern architects took such notions as place, identity and history from the dunghill of architectural history where they had ended up after the First World War. For Charles Jencks, the spiritual father of postmodernism, there was also the concept of 'double coding'. For example by inventively locking into tradition postmodern architecture, unlike modern architecture, was not just something for critics and connoisseurs but also for the public at large.

With his 'Rats, Posts and Other Pests' piece and other lectures and articles, Van Eyck set the pace of the Dutch discourse on postmodernism but he was also offering an alternative, namely the pre-war heroes of the Modern Movement in architecture. Tirelessly stressing the lasting value of the work of the Great Gang – he regarded Johannes Duiker, the designer of Zonnestraal, as the world's greatest architect – he pointed the latest batch of architects back in the direction of the early moderns.

Not just architecture students but also older architects already in practice were impressed by the tirades of the self-proclaimed conscience of Dutch architecture. At all events, Damascene conversions such as those that befell Michael Graves and Adolfo Natalini, both of whom exchanged modernism for postmodernism in around 1980, were unheard of in the Dutch architectural world.

Only a handful of renegade architects failed to be intimidated by Aldo van Eyck. One was Cees Dam, who even as a student at the Amsterdam Academy of Architecture was unimpressed by Van Eyck's structuralism. The combined city hall and opera house in Amsterdam designed with Wilhelm Holzbauer and completed in 1986 shows that he was not afraid of what Van Eyck called 'fascist' monumentalism. Nor was Dam averse to a mild post-modernism: his 1987 building for the Amsterdam Options Exchange looks like an updated version of an Italian Renaissance palazzo.

Carel Weeber, Dutch architecture's *enfant terrible*, was equally unfazed by Van Eyck. Indeed, he labelled the labyrinthine architecture of Hertzberger, Van Eyck and their followers the 'New Frumpishness' (Nieuwe Truttigheid) and argued for a 'rationalist' architecture and urbanism of monolithic perimeter blocks. In his master plan for Venserpolder in Amsterdam, where he himself designed a block, Weeber showed a different way of doing it. His urbanism proved to be a return to that of the pre-modern era, before Van Eyck's Great Gang existed, and in that respect was itself essentially postmodern.

Social Housing for Young People Rotterdam

Mecanoo 1985

The careers of four Delft architecture students got off to a flying start in 1980 when they won a competition held by a social housing corporation (Maatschappij voor Volkswoningen) for young people's accommodation on Kruisplein in Rotterdam. Completed five years later by what was now the Mecanoo practice, the design was the architects' reaction to the shabby urban renewal then in full swing in the major Dutch cities. Mecanoo's first built work is an early example of neo- or schoolteachers' modernism, a style popular in the 1980s particularly among young architects who had studied in Delft.
The two-part ensemble of assorted dwellings types and shops marks a return to early modernism. Now in a fairly shabby state, it looks more like something from the early 1960s when modernism was the prevailing style in this country.

City Theatre Rotterdam

Wim Quist 1988

The 1980s saw Wim Quist assembling an impressive oeuvre of museums, banks and other prestigious buildings. All exhibit his predilection for stern, simple geometric forms. His city theatre in Rotterdam, dubbed 'de kist van Quist' (Quist's box), is dominated visually by boxes: the ribs of another three are slung from the rectangular front facade. Quist, who was Government Architect from 1975 to 1979, was regarded abroad as the pre-eminent representative of Dutch architecture, characterized as this was, apparently, by a Calvinist simplicity. But even when the economic crisis of the 1980s made poor man's architecture the norm, there was still no such single entity as 'Dutch architecture'. At all events, the greyness of another prolific Dutch architect, Herman Hertzberger, was far more complex than that of Quist.

ROTTERDAMSE
SCHOUWBURG
AMEN DE TOUR KIJKEN
29 JUNI T/M 21 JULI
GRATIS ENTREE
Ontmoet
elkaar in de
OPEN

De Peperklip Rotterdam

Carel Weeber 1982

'I'm the last architect to have given form to social housing as it was meant to be', architect Carel Weeber once said about De Peperklip and De Zwarte Madonna, his large ceramic tile-clad housing blocks in Rotterdam and The Hague respectively. 'They're safety nets for people who can't find and afford a home, and that's what they look like: tenements.' Weeber's 'rationalist' superblocks hark back to the pre-modern urbanism of perimeter blocks and as such are an antidote to the 'New Frumpishness' of structuralism. The 'Black Madonna' of 1985 has since been demolished. That particular tenement stood in the centre of The Hague, for which plans came and went, generally only partly executed if at all. Twenty years on, Weeber's 'state architecture' no longer rhymed with the new ideas of the city's administrators and the social rented units of De Zwarte Madonna had to make way for towers of offices and swish apartments.

MORS Company Building Opmeer

Benthem Crouwel Architekten 1988

Jan Benthem and Mels Crouwel began their career in the 1980s as confirmed functionalists. 'If it's functional, it's beautiful', they aver in their contribution to the celebrated symposium 'How modern is Dutch architecture?', with which Rem Koolhaas took his leave as professor at Delft University of Technology in 1990. And yet this early building in Opmeer in the province of North Holland is proof that a design is not just the outcome of a client's brief. Benthem and Crouwel could have met the demands made by the company commissioning the building in so many ways. But they were among the few Dutch architects to opt for a high-tech approach, with many steel structural components left in sight. And why was that? Because it looked good.

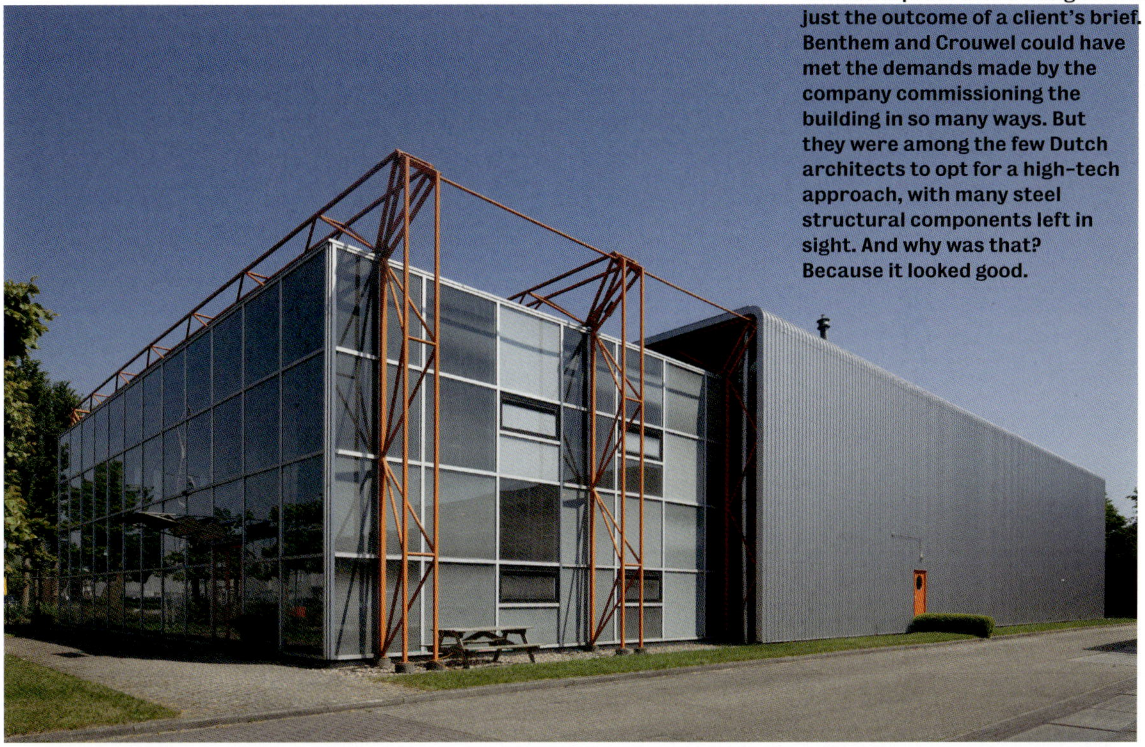

City Hall Lelystad

Jan Hoogstad 1984

As with Wim Quist, Jan Hoogstad's work has also been described as neo-rationalist. Yet his buildings show that there can be major differences within neo-rationalism. Hoogstad is a master of exaggeration. His buildings are at times every bit as outlandish as the modernist behemoths built in the 1970s and 1980s in the Eastern Bloc and now valued for their over-the-top ugliness.
By the same token, Lelystad Town Hall with its cascading front facade stands a better chance of being appreciated now than when it was completed in 1984.

Apollo Schools

Amsterdam

Herman Hertzberger 1983

In the 1970s Herman Hertzberger, who to his great displeasure had become known as a structuralist, developed a keen interest in school buildings. Schools could satisfy to perfection his great concern for designing places that incite encounter.
The schools Hertzberger designed on Apollolaan in Amsterdam have nothing of the traditional type with classrooms lining corridors. In one of the two schools, classrooms assemble in a spiral about an atrium that does duty as a roofed schoolyard. Stairs are a strong presence in the school. More than just a means of bridging differences in height, they are invitations to sit or hang out. The Apollo schools date from a time when grey concrete block was the norm in Hertzberger's architecture.

Extension to ESTEC

Noordwijk

Aldo van Eyck 1989

Like Van Eyck's first large structuralist building, the orphanage in Amsterdam (1960), his extension to the European Space Agency in Noordwijk can be best seen from the air. From there it is easy to observe the development of Van Eyck's structuralism. If the orphanage is assembled from many small and a few large boxes with domes, the ESTEC facilities building is much more of a single fluid entity, whose almost complete symmetry brings to mind a flower.
Another major difference between the early and late work of Aldo van Eyck is the use of colours. Unlike the all-grey orphanage his ESTEC building is multi-hued. 'The rainbow is my favourite colour', Van Eyck once said.

OPERA
OPERA
O.T.
Georg Friedrich Händel
Samson

City Hall and Opera House Amsterdam

Cees Dam and Wilhelm Holzbauer 1986

Known in Amsterdam as the 'Stopera', this combination of city hall (*stadshuis*) and opera house has a long and dramatic history. Not only was there a great deal of political wrangling about budgetary overruns, construction of the monumental ensemble on Waterlooplein met with fierce public opposition. In the world of architecture, its design precipitated an unprecedented barrage of criticism against one of the architects, Cees Dam.

Aldo van Eyck, the self-proclaimed conscience of Dutch architecture, denounced the design in various newspapers and professional magazines. His influential polemics were typical of the architectural climate in the 1980s. Its monumentality brought Van Eyck to label the Stopera a 'politically incorrect' building. Incorrect in a moral sense, that is: he made a connection between the Stopera and the work of Albert Speer, Adolf Hitler's chief architect. Postmodernism also felt the lash of Van Eyck's tongue. To his mind this was even less politically correct than the Stopera.

Motorwal Amsterdam

OMA/Rem Koolhaas 1987

With their 1982 urban master plan for IJplein in Amsterdam-Noord, OMA and Rem Koolhaas demonstrated how the heritage of the Modern Movement could be reused. On a disused shipbuilding site in the north of Amsterdam, OMA projected 22 famous modernist designs for housing estates by the likes of Ludwig Hilberseimer, Johannes Duiker and Lotte Stam-Beese. From these they distilled an urban design that seemed to date from the 1920s, the Heroic Age of modernism. Motorwal, a complex of dwellings, shops and a community centre and the only building at IJplein designed by OMA themselves, quotes from the modernist heritage. For example, the stairs doubling back derive from J.P. Kloos's block of suspended bridge maisonettes of 1970 in the Osdorp area of Amsterdam. And the building stands on pilotis, as prescribed by Le Corbusier in his *Les cinq points de l'architecture moderne* (1927).

Right and Wrong

Chapter 2

'How modern is Dutch architecture?' was the title of the lecture with which Rem Koolhaas marked his retirement as professor at Delft University of Technology in 1990. In the farewell address with which he opened the symposium, Koolhaas lashed out at the Dutch architecture of that time. By then the Netherlands' most famous architect, he concluded that the Modern Movement of the 'Heroic Age' between the two wars was still the major source of inspiration particularly among young architects. The second half of the 1980s had seen buildings erected throughout the Netherlands whose flat roofs, glazed exteriors and unembellished rendered walls referred to the work of such pioneers of modernism as Le Corbusier, Ludwig Mies van der Rohe and Alvar Aalto.

Koolhaas was shocked: 'How is it possible for Christ's sake that in a century informed entirely by instability and change, in the art form best equipped to reflect society, and in a language, that of architecture, celebrated especially for its capacity for transformation – that despite all this, buildings ranging over a hundred-year period still look so much alike?'

He also failed to understand the lack of an 'ideological response' to the fall of the Berlin Wall in 1989 and the disappearance of really existing socialism, 'which in almost all cases has latently nourished and provided the justification for our modern architecture'.

Koolhaas's words expressed a great faith in the workings of the Zeitgeist. Each period requires its own architecture, he reasoned, and so architecture that harked back to earlier periods is 'shockingly' anachronistic.

Some young architects rejected Koolhaas's criticism. Ben van Berkel, for one, explained at the symposium that as an architect he had been shaped less by the Modern Movement than by television, music, shopping centres and the first moon landing. And Erick van Egeraat then of Mecanoo gave the ball back to Koolhaas by accusing him of sending an entire generation of architects out on the Modern Movement trail.

No matter how hard the young architects fought back, however, Koolhaas's assertion that they seemed mainly to be living in the modernist past was confirmed by the Dutch entry to the Venice Architecture Biennale of 1991. This exhibition, significantly entitled 'Modernism without Dogma', showed how ten emerging Dutch architecture offices including Mecanoo, DKV and Benthem Crouwel drew freely from the modernist panoply of forms. In the words of Hans Ibelings, the exhibition's curator and then working at the Netherlands Architecture Institute, 'There is no question of a generation gap, nor are the young architects committing "intellectual patricide".'

And yet Koolhaas hadn't got it completely right. The work of those ten new Dutch practices was not a repeat of heroic modernism as he had suggested. There was nothing among the young architects of the often socialist-tinted idealism of the old modernists – functional white buildings for a better world together: their modernism was a 'modernism without dogma'. What was contemporary about the new Dutch architecture was that it drew freely on old forms without the social commitment that went with them in former times.

But it was this very lack of commitment in neo-modernism that troubled Koolhaas. 'Triumphalist' he called it, 'utterly non-dangerous, toothless, sterile'. Ibelings on the other hand praised 'the liberal and unencumbered involvement with the architecture of the recent past . . . , inventive and with a tremendous richness of form.'

As for the reasons for modernism's resurgence, Koolhaas and Ibelings remain silent. Not so Hans van Dijk, the most important Dutch architecture critic of the 1980s. In a number of articles written in the early 1990s he explained that only in the Netherlands had modernism had enjoyed an unbroken tradition in the twentieth century. Outside of the Soviet Union and Germany, ours was the only country where modern architecture became a fully fledged 'movement' in the 1920s. But whereas modernism was given short shrift in Germany by the Nazis and in the Soviet Union by the Stalinists, it continued unhindered in this country. That said, the modernists were, according to Van Dijk, continually obliged to defend their stance, in the 1930s against that of Groep '32, a splinter group that called for a return to decoration and classicism, and after the Second World War against the traditionalists of the Delft School such as Granpré Molière and Berghoef. The upshot was that 'each generation took up modern architecture as a polemic project, recapitulating its departure-points in all their ideological purity.'

It was only after Granpré Molière retired as Delft architecture professor in 1953 that the traditionalist opposition eased off, so Van Dijk tells us. By 1970 modernism had been fully accepted, not just at the architecture schools but also by clients. Thereafter, according to Van Dijk, there was no need for the modernists to prove themselves: 'Classicism and traditionalism, the old enemies of modern architecture, had been vanquished and the new enemies, populism and postmodernism, had been shut out.'

Given the lack of 'dangerous enemies or inspirational revival movements', modernism degenerated into what Van Dijk dubbed 'schoolteachers' modernism'. With no further need to justify itself, modernism was no longer an intellectual tradition but a tradition of forms mainly passed on by professors of architecture at Delft University of Technology. But although by the turn of the 1990s no one believed in the dogmas of the early moderns or in the 'feasibility of an egalitarian and just society', there was nevertheless, in Van Dijk's words, 'an almost intuitive awareness of what was acceptable in architecture and what was not'.

Put another way, a lack of dogma didn't mean that by the early 1990s moralism in Dutch architecture had been put to rest. Broadly speaking, moralism at that time amounted to the following: flat roofs and ribbon glazing are 'good' because they were introduced by architects who wanted to make the world a better place, pitched roofs and postmodern pillars are 'bad' because Nazi architect Albert Speer and Aldo van Eyck's 'Rats and Pests' used them.

Even an outsider like Charles Jencks observed a link between the absence of postmodernism in Dutch architecture and the Second World War. In an interview in 1993, Jencks gave five reasons why postmodernism had almost entirely by-passed the Netherlands: 'First off, there was in the Netherlands, and perhaps still is, the general European trauma of the First and Second World Wars. The white modern architecture is a metaphor for healing, for health. You thought that if your country were to change into one huge hospital, one huge Zonnestraal, everyone would heal and everything would turn out fine. Another cause is the reaction to the Second World War. Modernism was the anti-fascist style, just as communism was the anti-fascist ideology. The Dutch bought into the idea that by being modern they would not be nationalist, not be reactionary, not be repressive, not be anti-democratic. Third, the Dutch more than any other nation are "homines economici": if it's not cheap it can't be good. If you can't justify a thing here in terms of its usefulness, the deal's off. Fourth, Calvinism still looms large in the Netherlands. And modernism is the ultimate Calvinist, Puritan architecture. If Calvin had lived in the twentieth century, his name would have been Mies van der Calvin. Lastly, the welfare state and the dream of social equality work better in the Netherlands than in most other countries. That explains why there's no real need here for postmodernism, the way there isn't in the Scandinavian countries.'

Jencks was critical of modernism in the Netherlands and concluded that there was a downside to it: 'Your country took the modernist Voltaire's advice to cultivate one's garden seriously. That's one of your blessings but it also has a dark side. Take the bulb fields. These are concentration camps for tulips and carry man's control over nature to absurd lengths. Look at the tulips and you can see them as people. The hospital modernism of architects like Van der Vlugt and Duiker has a dark side too. The drive to good health, the triumph of jogging, also had a big part to play in Nazi organizations like Kraft durch Freude. Modernism shares with National Socialism the obsession with the mechanical and with having control. The aircraft shown in Le Corbusier's books as examples for the new architecture stand for freedom but also represent the Luftwaffe.'

Just how schoolteachers' modernism prevailed at the architecture schools was made clear by Carel Weeber, who for many years taught at Delft's Faculty of Architecture, in an interview he gave in 1997. 'They still train state architects here in Delft. The students even now get bombarded with the Modern Movement of the twenties and thirties – this will change only when the current generation of professors retires.'

With modernism without dogma, neo-modernism, schoolteachers' modernism or whatever else you like to call it as its salient trend, Dutch architecture seemed out of step with the rest of the world. Postmodernism, which emerged in the 1980s most notably in the UK, the US and France, pretty well gave this country a miss, also in the years around 1990. Organic buildings like Alberts & Van Huut's NMB bank headquarters or the whoopee architecture of Sjoerd Soeters were incidents. Any modern classicist building that did get built was undoubtedly a mansion by an anonymous Dutch architect in an upmarket residential area such as Baarn or Wassenaar, or urban renewal to a design by the non-Dutch likes of Charles Vandenhove.

And so the Netherlands became the Cuba of modern architecture. And just as the Cuban communists were proud of the fact that their country was one of the last bastions of orthodox communism, so Dutch architects boasted that something as wretched as postmodernism could never take root in their country.

But in fact neo-modernism was little more than a typically Dutch, moralistic take on postmodernism. The modernists without dogma essentially were doing the same thing as the foreign postmodernists they despised, namely helping themselves liberally to architectural history. They just limited their scope out of moral considerations to that of the years 1920–1933, the brief period that for them had an air of 'rightness' about it, whereas the foreign postmodernists plundered the entire history of architecture, up to and including what was regarded as 'wrong'.

Hillekop Rotterdam

Mecanoo 1989

If one built design is proof that neo- or schoolteachers' modernism is essentially the Dutch strain of postmodernism, it's Mecanoo's Hillekop housing. The tallest and most striking component is a tower, which with its curved grid-like exterior closely resembles the apartment building of 1953 by Finnish modernist Alvar Aalto in the Neue Vahr district of Bremen, Germany.

The Hillekop tower also shows that the taste among Dutch neo-modernists broadened over time. If at first the 'heroic' modernism of the interwar years of architects like Le Corbusier and Berthold Lubetkin had been their key source of inspiration, later they quoted from post-war modernism as well.

Natal Rotterdam
Frits van Dongen 1990

'Aesthetic pragmatism' was how the critic Hans van Dijk described the Dutch architecture of the early 1990s. Then, as always, aesthetics proved to be subject to fashion. In the mid-1990s Van Dijk and other critics simultaneously drew attention to the fashion attributes with which architects had adorned their buildings in the preceding years.
That said, fashionable is still a dirty word in the architectural world. Although most architects want to be of their time, they also want their buildings to be timeless, simply because buildings are on site for many years if not permanently. The two have proved to be incompatible. Contemporaneity wins every time: all architecture is fashion-bound and can be easily dated from characteristics typical of that age. One of the architectural fashions of the early 1990s was the serpentine building, such as this Rotterdam housing block with shops designed by Frits van Dongen. This and other serpentine designs of those years were themselves examples of postmodern *citazionismo*: like his colleagues Van Dongen was familiar with the undulating Copan Building in São Paulo by the flamboyant Brazilian modernist Oscar Niemeyer.

Museum Boijmans Van Beuningen Pavilion Rotterdam

Hubert-Jan Henket 1991

Although Hubert-Jan Henket is older than most neo-modernists of the years around 1990, he also regarded himself as an heir to what he then called the Modern Movement and these days modernity. He considered the ideas of the modernists and their functionalist approach in particular to be just as relevant at century's end. Like Aldo van Eyck he was a great admirer of Johannes Duiker, the Dutch modernist who had taken the precept 'less is more' to an extreme in his Zonnestraal Sanatorium (1928).
Henket's pavilion for industrial design at Museum Boijmans Van Beuningen therefore belongs in the tradition of glass modernist buildings like Zonnestraal and Ludwig Mies van der Rohe's Farnsworth House (1951). Later the pavilion was largely redesignated as the museum café. This was not appreciated by Henket, who as a confirmed functionalist felt that a pavilion designed as an exhibition space could never do duty as a café.

Arts Academy Extension Maastricht

Wiel Arets 1993

On the strength of its elementary forms – three concrete and glass boxes interconnected by an aerial walkway – you might describe Wiel Arets's Arts Academy (Academie Beeldende Kunsten) extension in Maastricht as neo-modernist. But there is one key aspect of the Academy building that is anything but modernist: it is entirely opaque. Transparency was an obsession mainly among early German modernists like Ludwig Mies van der Rohe and Walter Gropius. For example, the workshop wing – a simple box – of the latter's Bauhaus building in Dessau of 1926 has a glass curtain wall, which lets passers-by observe what is happening inside. Yet although allied to the Bauhaus in terms of form and simplicity, the Academy building conceals all its indoor activity behind a glass-block exterior. The one exception is in the evening, when the building on Herdenkingsplein is lit up and silhouettes of its occupants can be seen.

Tweebos Dwars

Rotterdam

DKV 1993

Following Hillekop and Natal, Tweebos Dwars by DKV (Dolf Dobbelaar, Herman de Kovel and Paul de Vroom) is the third large neo-modernist urban renewal project in Rotterdam. All three complexes are light years away from the usual 1980s urban renewal, which took its cue from the existing surroundings. This generally followed the old street pattern of the neighbourhood but also adhered to its neighbours in terms of scale (usually four storeys) and material (brick). The neo-modernists jettisoned this habit, much as the modernists had done seventy years earlier. Their architecture as well as their urbanism marked a return to the modernist's tabula rasa principle. Thus in Tweebos Dwars, DKV replaced two perimeter blocks with an ensemble of modernist rows and free-standing towers either side of a traffic-free plaza, bringing 'light, air and space' into an old part of town.

Haans Office Building Tilburg

Jo Coenen 1992

The offices for Haans, the Tilburg entrepreneur for whom Jo Coenen also designed a villa, adorned the cover of the *Architecture in the Netherlands Yearbook 1992/93.* First published in 1987, the *Yearbook* soon grew into an institution. For architects it is important that their work is in it not just for the privilege, but also because the *Yearbook* is used by councillors and other clients looking for architects. This has created a new category in Dutch architecture: the *Yearbook* architects, the lucky ones with an official stamp of approval.
In recent instalments of the *Yearbook* the choice of building on the front cover has become increasingly important and is kept secret until the presentation. The chosen building is then proclaimed national champion in architecture. With hindsight, the Haans office was the Dutch architecture champion of the 1992–1993 season.

Karbouw Office Building Amersfoort

Van Berkel & Bos Architectuurbureau 1992

Right angles are few and far between in Ben van Berkel's company building for Karbouw; and, except for the ribs of the aluminium cladding panels, there are few parallel lines. This clearly places it in the realm of Deconstructivism, the style that the Museum of Modern Art in New York sought to elevate to the New International Style with a major exhibition in 1988. That said, the building is a typically Dutch representative of Deconstructivism. Other than in the designs of the style's pioneers such as Zaha Hadid and Coop Himmelb(l)au, the clashing geometries give no impression of instability or insecurity. The black band on which the building seems to rest is a regular base. But above all it is the continuation of the swelling line of the office roof into the flank walls of the workplace that lends the building cohesion and unity.

entree
Express Service

West Terminal Schiphol

Benthem Crouwel Architekten 1993

Benthem Crouwel became house architect to Schiphol International Airport, the airport that swelled in the 1980s and 1990s into a full-scale city where people live in its hotels, work in its offices and do their shopping in its stores. The functionalist approach to architecture taken by Benthem Crouwel proved eminently suitable for enlarging Schiphol, which besides playing at being a city is first and foremost a gigantic logistics machine that brings flows of people and goods from one place to another.

In view of its endorsement by travellers – year in and year out it scores high in the list of 'world's best airports' – Schiphol is a well-run machine. One disadvantage of being a machine is that Schiphol, like so many international airports, has become a non-place.

City Hall and Library The Hague

Richard Meier 1995

In the 1980s, when Dutch neo-modernism was on the rise, the American Richard Meier (b. 1934) was the 'architect's architect' in this country. He had shown us the way: as a member of the New York Five, a quintet of New York neo-modernists, his work in the late 1960s allied him with Le Corbusier, Giuseppe Terragni and other pioneers of the Modern Movement. Meier is the only one of the Five to remain faithful to neo-modernism. The other New Yorkers took it as a stepping-off point for the most wildly diverse work. Peter Eisenman for example discovered a new French philosopher (Jacques Derrida, Gilles Deleuze) every ten years or so and a new style to go with it. And Michael Graves, who in 1998 would transform a modernist office building not far from Meier's city hall into Castalia, inspired by old Dutch canal houses, converted to postmodernism at the end of the 1970s.
The history of Meier's city hall was accompanied by a heated argument between two of the city's aldermen. Adri Duivesteijn backed Meier's design whereas his colleague Gerard van Otterloo wanted the one by Rem Koolhaas. The squabbling ended with both aldermen resigning and Meier's design being the one built.
Soon after being taken into use Meier's city hall was dubbed the 'Ice Palace' because of its dazzling expanse of white.

Extension to the House of Representatives

The Hague

Pi de Bruijn 1992

In 1980 Pi de Bruijn won the invited competition to enlarge the lower house of the Dutch parliament. It took all of 12 years to get the new build in place.
De Bruijn's design admits to an element of monumentality, which came under criticism in the architectural world. 'In the magazine *Archis* the critic Geert Bekaert described the extension as questionable', said Pi de Bruijn looking back at that criticism in an interview in 2009: 'The discussion was a knife in my back. I lost friends because of it. They started giving me a wide berth.'
According to De Bruijn, Dutch architecture was little different in 2009: 'The situation in architecture in this country still amounts to a kind of Calvinist sect. Every so often you get assessed and they consider whether you're acting honestly.'

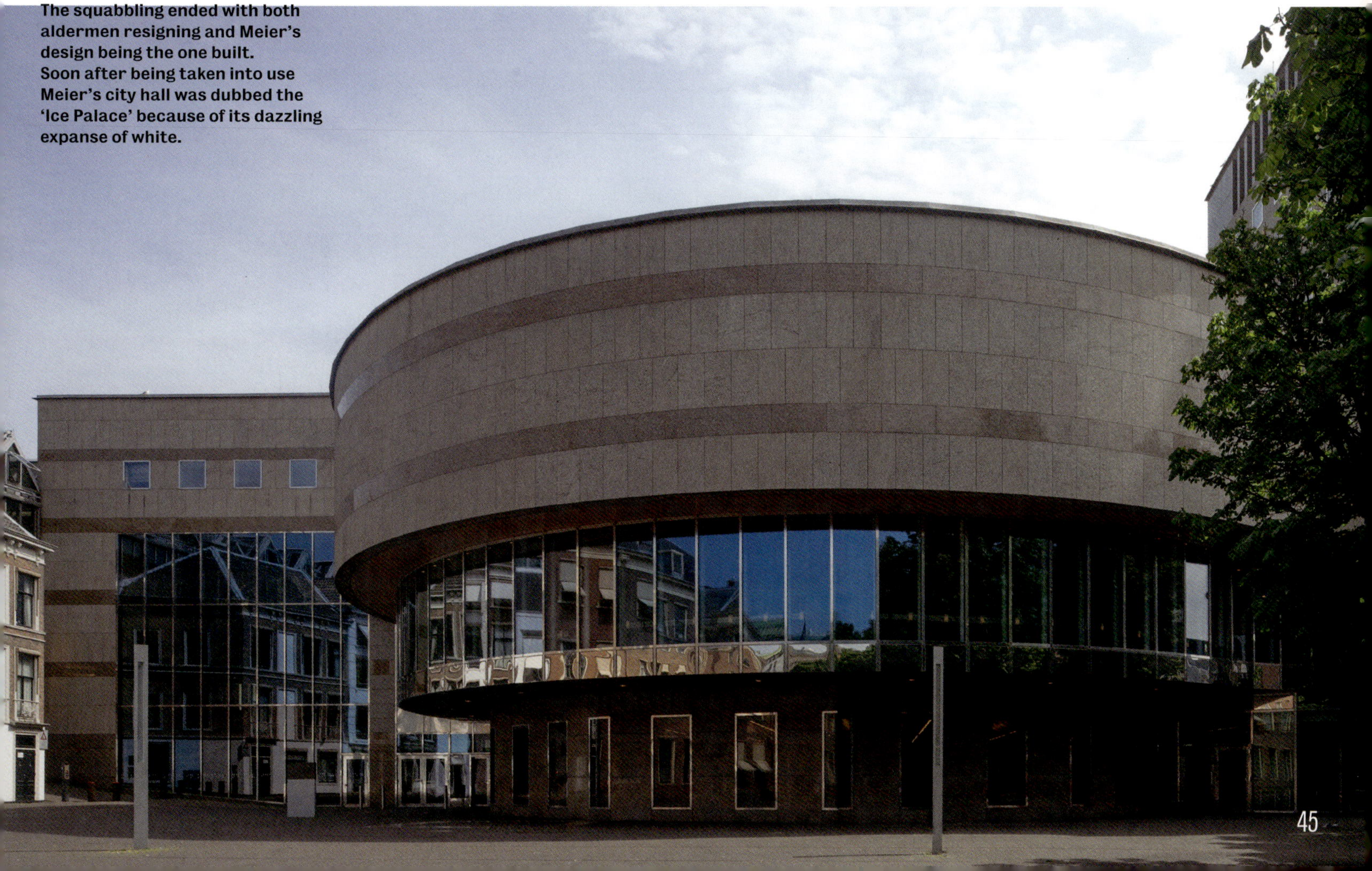

Library Almelo

Mecanoo 1994

If Mecanoo were pioneers of neo-modernism in the years around 1990, they were later exponents of collage architecture in the mid-1990s when that was briefly in vogue in the Netherlands. In the Almelo library, Mecanoo literally exploded the modernist box resulting in a riot of forms, colours and materials and a capricious floor plan.
The explosion of neo-modernism ushered in a gradual exodus from Mecanoo. Soon after the library was completed Erick van Egeraat left the practice to develop his own highly personal form of neo-baroque. Four years later it was the turn of Chris de Wijer, followed, after a further four years, by Henk Döll. As Roelf Steenhuis had left Mecanoo back in the late 1980s, the only remaining member of the original quintet since 2003 is Francine Houben.

Double Dutch

Chapter 3

Pay a visit first to Mecanoo's Kruisplein housing in Rotterdam and then to their library in Almelo and it's hard to believe they were designed by the same practice. The young people's building is a respectable block of flats in the tradition of the modernism of architects like J.J.P. Oud, who designed Almelo's town hall not a stone's throw from the library. Yet the library has nothing in common with the late modernism of Oud's city hall. With its curiously angled zinc roof, curving copper wall, concrete piers fanning out and a dazzling blue glazed facade, the building is a riot of forms and materials.

Mecanoo's young people's housing (1985) and their library (1994) show that Dutch architecture had changed dramatically since Rem Koolhaas's lambasting of neo-modernism in 1991. Once the champions of neo-modernism, the members of Mecanoo were now collage architects. And they weren't the only ones. Other Dutch architects, such as Jo Coenen with his Netherlands Architecture Institute in Rotterdam (1993) and Rudy Uytenhaak with his House for Fine Arts in Apeldoorn (1995), designed buildings in the 1990s that exhibited a clash of disparate forms and materials. But it took a foreign architect to dish up the most heterogeneous collage in the Netherlands, to wit the Groninger Museum in Groningen (1994). The Italian Alessandro Mendini enlisted four foreign architects to design one pavilion apiece in different materials and colours to create this unabashedly postmodern building.

So collage architecture was not an exclusively Dutch phenomenon. As early as 1988, the Museum of Modern Art in New York had mounted the exhibition 'Deconstructivist Architecture' in an endeavour to proclaim as the New International Style the fragmented architecture of Daniel Libeskind, Zaha Hadid, Peter Eisenman and others under the name Deconstructivism. One of the exhibition's curators was the grand old man of American architecture Philip Johnson (1906–2005). With 'Deconstructivist Architecture' he hoped to repeat the success of his earlier MoMA exhibition 'The International Style' (1932). As befits the introduction of a new style of architecture, the exhibition's curators sought to justify the train-wreck architecture of the exhibitors. The bottom line was that the Zeitgeist called for fragmentation. At the close of the second millennium globalization and digitization were changing the world at an increasingly furious pace and with the times more uncertain than ever, the appropriate architectural expression, the curators argued, was Deconstructivism.

Rem Koolhaas was another to take part in the MoMA exhibition. Later, he would distance himself from Decon by disqualifying it as a banal illustration of the uncertain spirit of the times. All the same, his Dans Theater in The Hague (1987) and the Kunsthal in Rotterdam (1992), the building that marked his international breakthrough as an active architect, make him a pioneer of Dutch 'train-wreck' architecture.

Dutch Decon was soft when compared with that of Eisenman and Hadid. Razor-sharp and unpractical forms such as those found in Eisenman are absent: the Dutch designers of one-over-the-eight architecture were never roaring drunk, just a bit tiddly if anything. And unlike Eisenman they scarcely ever enlisted the aid of French thinkers like Jacques Derrida and Gilles Deleuze to explain their work. A docile Decon without dogma is one way of characterizing the Dutch collage architecture of around 1995, the successor of neo-modernism.

The anything-goes approach of Dutch collage architecture made it especially fashionable. Critics had little difficulty in identifying elements that the collage architects repeatedly used, such as non-traditional cladding materials like zinc, corrugated sheet and exotic wood types, tilting facade planes and stand-alone perforated screens. It was for this type of architecture that critic Hans van Dijk invented the term 'aesthetic pragmatism' in an essay in the *Architecture in the Netherlands Yearbook 1994/95*. 'We are builders', he has the Dutch architects of the mid-1990s say. 'We have soberly accepted the programme of requirements . . . But we do want it to look as good as possible.' And, as always, 'good' in the mid-1990s is commensurate with the spirit (read: the architectural fashion) of the times.

Decon was not the only architectural style in the 1990s that drew its *raison d'être* from the spirit of the times. The onset of the decade, when the internet and digital design were still in their infancy, saw the emergence of complex amoeboid buildings designed using computer techniques. These were soon dubbed 'blobs' (from Binary Large Objects, originally amorphous chunks of data), to the displeasure of the designers themselves.

Computer architects like Ben van Berkel, Kas Oosterhuis and Lars Spuybroek took the following line of reasoning: When computers rule the world and all information can be sent all over the globe in no time, our understanding of time and space will change utterly. Even our understanding of reality won't be the same: the real reality will steadily be replaced by 'virtual reality' until it's no longer clear where one ends and the other begins.

All this had to have major consequences for architecture. The world, and therefore also architecture, was faced with a 'paradigm shift'. The world was becoming fluid and so was architecture - this was their reasoning in a nutshell.

Kas Oosterhuis, himself an international pioneer in computer architecture, went a step further: he believed that buildings in the digital age would become interactive and 'alive'. His own Salt Water Pavilion on Neeltje Jans 'work island' in Zeeland is an organic, fluid building where colour projections and water flows respond to the movement of visitors. Lars Spuybroek was another to realize a number of interactive works. Since 2004 the town of Doetinchem near the German border has been home to the D-Tower, a colossal sculpted teardrop designed by Spuybroek and the artist Q.S. Serafijn that changes colour in response to the daily mood of townsfolk as relayed in an online inquiry. And in Son en Breugel, near Eindhoven, there is the Son-O-House (2004), designed by Spuybroek's firm NOX, a sinuous structure containing a sound work, composed by Edwin van der Heide, whose patterns are shaped by, once again, the movements of visitors.

But most blobs, certainly if designed by architects who don't necessarily believe that the digital age would be accompanied by a paradigm shift and who regard computer-aided design mainly as a handy resource, are static, unwieldy monoliths. The copper-clad pop/rock venue Mezz in Breda (2002), for example, designed by Erick van Egeraat, the Mecanoo man who set up in independent practice in 1995, is a beached whale. And the film theatre designed in 2000 by another Mecanoo architect, Francine Houben, as part of the extension to the Open Air Museum in Arnhem, became a gigantic brass boulder.

So it transpired that the spirit of the times at millennium's end spoke double Dutch, quite literally. Comparable appeals to the Zeitgeist gave rise to two utterly different types of architecture. If the credo of the computer architects ('the world is becoming fluid and so is architecture') elicited amoebic monoliths, that of the Deconstructivists ('the world is chaotic and so is architecture') brought collages of fragments.

Nederlands Dans Theater The Hague

OMA/Rem Koolhaas 1987

Rem Koolhaas is the fashion king of Dutch architecture who has launched many new fashions, major and minor. He introduced the forward-tilting facade and the floor that becomes a ceiling into the end-of-century Dutch architecture as well as the collage. At the start of the 1980s Koolhaas, together with Aldo van Eyck, pointed young architects in the direction of early modernism. In the middle of that decade, however, when they started taking his advice, he had already moved on to something entirely different: the collage-like Dans Theater in The Hague. Getting this, Koolhaas's first big building, onto site was a long and laborious process. In 1980 it was slated to stand alongside the Circustheater in coastal Scheveningen, but in 1984 the City of The Hague decided that it was to be combined with a concert hall on Spui in the city centre. In the meantime Koolhaas's theatre had lost its arch, which had been lifted from Le Corbusier's unrealized design for the Palace of the Soviets (1931). It did retain another reference: the undulating roof is taken from the school Antoni Gaudí built alongside his Sagrada Família church in Barcelona.

Lucent Danstheater

Kunsthal Rotterdam
OMA/Rem Koolhaas 1992

In 2012, when the *Architecture in the Netherlands Yearbook* reached its 25th edition, the then editors chose Rem Koolhaas's Kunsthal as the best Dutch building of the past 25 years. Interestingly in that respect, it was Jo Coenen's Haans office in Tilburg that graced the cover of the 1993 *Yearbook*, the edition that also included the Kunsthal.
The choice of the Kunsthal was an acknowledgement of Koolhaas as the country's number one architect. As the father of conceptual architecture, he has influenced many architects at home and abroad and has earned Dutch architecture a huge reputation.
In terms of use, the Kunsthal has proved a difficult and somewhat unpractical building for exhibition curators and visitors alike. But for those editors of the *Yearbook* this shortcoming was more than compensated for by the complexity of the interior with its ramps in various directions.
Although Koolhaas railed against Dutch neo-modernism in the opening speech at the 1990 symposium marking his retirement as professor at Delft University of Technology, the Kunsthal itself refers to the work of early moderns, such as Konstantin Melnikov's Soviet Pavilion at the 1925 Exposition des Arts Décoratifs in Paris and Ludwig Mies van der Rohe's post-war work in steel and glass.

Netherlands Architecture Institute Rotterdam

Jo Coenen 1993

Founded in 1988, the Netherlands Architecture Institute or NAI was formed by combining three institutes, the Netherlands Architecture Documentation Centre (NDB), the Architecture Museum Foundation (SAM) and Stichting Wonen. Five years later it moved into premises of its own. In accordance with the architectural fashion of those years, the building designed by Jo Coenen was a collage of three distinct volumes. The archive was housed in the 'banana', an elongated curved portion, the offices in a glass box slung from a 'drying rack' and the exhibition areas in a concrete box. The NAI once proudly presented itself as the 'world's largest architecture institute'. The building symbolized the success of the Dutch architecture policy of central government, provinces and municipalities. Just as symbolic is that the NAI was discontinued on 1 January 2013 and itself made part of what is now The New Institute. In the intervening quarter of a century Dutch architecture had flourished as never before, partly thanks to the NAI.

Neeltje Jans Water Pavilions

Oosterhuis Associates and NOX 1997

The freshwater and salt water pavilions lie like a stranded giant sea snake on the former Delta Works construction island (Neeltje Jans) in the waters of Westerschelde. The black, somewhat angular salt water pavilion, designed by Kas Oosterhuis, hangs slightly over the water as if about to re-enter it. Not that this is possible, since its tail, the shiny freshwater pavilion half covered with sand from the dunes, seems rooted to the shore. It is no coincidence that the two pavilions suggest a marine creature. Kas Oosterhuis in particular believes that architecture in the digital age will increasingly resemble a living organism. The two pavilions are a foretaste of this development. Not only do they have exclusively curving organic forms and a blurred distinction between floors, walls and ceilings thanks to digital design and building techniques, their exhibitions on saline and fresh water are interactive. Light projections, water flows and sounds respond to the movements made by visitors.

Groninger Museum Groningen

Alessandro Mendini 1994

A perversity – this is critic Hans van Dijk writing in 1994 about the new Groninger Museum. The chief architect of this overtly post-modernist collage, the Italian Alessandro Mendini, enlisted the services of four architects and designers amongst whom the Frenchman Philippe Starck and the Austrian duo Coop Himmelb(l)au. Each of the designers was responsible for a part of the museum. The result is an accumulation of heterogeneous volumes, varying from a Deconstructivist roof to a pillbox in the water. Another critic, Max van Rooy, denounced the museum as pandering to fashion and already behind the times at its completion. Postmodernism had long had its day, he contended, and the Groninger Museum was postmodernism in extremis. Now, 20 years on, we can say that the museum was not so much behind its time as ahead of it, a harbinger of what was in store for Dutch architecture.

Son-O-House Son en Breugel

NOX 2004

In Son-O-House, a sound sculpture on an industrial estate in Son en Breugel, outside Eindhoven, NOX (Lars Spuybroek) has elevated computer baroque to new heights. 'The house where sounds live' swirls in all directions, a pavilion assembled from curved ribs wrapped in a transparent skin. Like the pavilions on Neeltje Jans, Son-O-House is interactive. Twenty-three sensors register the movements of visitors, which are then transformed into sound. Four years after Son-O-House, Spuybroek, one of the pioneers of 'non-standard' architecture, closed down his NOX office and turned to theorizing on a new architecture as a university professor, most notably at the Georgia Institute of Technology in Atlanta. 'Architecture needs a breather, preferably a very long one', he said in an interview in 2012. In his book *The Sympathy of Things* (2011) he calls for a new decorative architecture based on an update of the theories of the nineteenth-century architectural historian John Ruskin.

Electrical Substation (REMU)

Amersfoort

Van Berkel en Bos 1994

With its gently fragmented configuration, Ben van Berkel's electrical substation in Amersfoort is a typically Dutch Deconstructivist building. A few years later Van Berkel's architecture would get increasingly fluid. One example is the pavilion he designed to house the 'RealSpace in QuickTimes' exhibition, on show for a couple of months in 1996 in the main room of the Netherlands Architecture Institute. The curved wooden panels composing the billowing construction were made using a computer-controlled milling machine.
Van Berkel and his office partner Caroline Bos saw the computer as a means of liberation from modernism, as we can read in *Move*, their 1999 monograph, whose thickness (834 pages) and profusion of essays and illustrations recall Koolhaas's *S,M,L,XL* (1995): 'Modernist architecture was all about mechanical techniques such as collage and montage', said Van Berkel when explaining his new-found freedom in an interview: 'The postmodernists are in fact doing exactly the same: they browse through the history of architecture and mechanically cobble together a design from the components they've chosen. It's only now, thanks to the computer, that we can dispense with montage. It's computers that enable us to erase the borders between components in architecture.'

House for the Fine Arts Apeldoorn

Rudy Uytenhaak 1995

In the Netherlands, the economic upturn in the years 1985–2008 was accompanied by an unprecedented flurry of building. While industrial estates and Vinex housing developments sprang up everywhere, the existing cultural infrastructure was itself given an overhaul. Virtually all large and medium-sized cities received new theatres, concert halls, libraries, pop/rock venues, art museums and museums in general. There was so much that at times the supply exceeded the demand. Pop/rock venues in particular found themselves in difficulties after moving into newly built premises. One such venue, Muzinq, a blob designed in Almere by the British architect Will Alsop, had to close its doors in 2005 after just three months as the occupier had gone bankrupt.
In 1995 it was Apeldoorn's turn to receive a new cultural centre bearing the archaic name House for the Fine Arts. Designed by Rudy Uytenhaak and housing five cultural institutions, it is a sterling example of Dutch Deconstructivism. The facades of the different clearly articulated volumes have their own cladding materials in what is a fairly sedate collage.

Chassé Theater Breda

Herman Hertzberger 1995

Rem Koolhaas's influence extended beyond younger architects to the likes of Herman Hertzberger. The older man stated on several occasions in the 1990s that Koolhaas had changed him as an architect. He has never been specific about the nature of Koolhaas's influence. It probably meant that Hertzberger was able to shake off his structuralist straitjacket.
The Chassé Theater illustrates Hertzberger's new freedom. He is no longer fazed by big statements. Spectacular undulating roofs draw the different building parts together. Inside, where Hertzberger has given as much thought to stairs and places as in his structuralist buildings, the most immediately striking aspect is the colour. No structuralist greyness here: the enormous columns in the foyers supporting the undulating roof are red and orange and the floor orange-red. And the chairs in the auditoria are red, the traditional theatre colour.

Mezz Breda

Erick van Egeraat 2002

Mezz is one of the many pop/rock venues to arrive in the Netherlands in the decades before and after 2000. It sees Erick van Egeraat enlarging an existing building, an officers' mess hall dating from 1889, with a copper-plated blob containing an auditorium for 650 fans.

Mezz is the complete opposite of the neo-modernist boxes Van Egeraat designed at the start of his career as a member of Mecanoo. In an interview he confessed that his dramatic change of style was partly prompted by personal circumstances. When visiting the Louvre in Paris with his new Russian wife and looking at length at the opulence of the wood-carvings in the Salon d'Apollon, she said, 'I hope you understand now that there's more than just white walls and glass.' Van Egeraat understood: he would never design a white box again. Indeed, Van Egeraat is one of the few architects today who unabashedly claim to aspire to beauty, an anathema in architecture since the rise of modernism.

Villa VPRO Hilversum

MVRDV 1997

Mecanoo's flying start in the 1980s would be eclipsed by that of MVRDV ten years later. Their first built work, new premises for the VPRO broadcasting organization in Hilversum's Media Park, was given extensive coverage in the architectural magazines even before it was completed.
Villa VPRO owes much to an unbuilt design in 1990 by OMA/Rem Koolhaas for the Zentrum für Kunst und Medientechnologie in Karlsruhe, Germany. Like Koolhaas's Zentrum, it is comprised of floors interconnected by stairs, steps, ramps and folds to form a single unbroken entity. The 'promenade architecturale' that can be taken across the sloping floors and stairs ends at a roof garden. Like Koolhaas's Kunsthal, the villa proved difficult to use. The VPRO staff suffered from a lack of privacy and poor acoustics. Such acoustic measures as carpets on the floor and sound-absorbing zeppelins in the tallest spaces have made the building more user-friendly.

Fuck the Context

Chapter 4

The collage architecture of the mid-1990s was a trend that didn't last long. For most architects, including Mecanoo, train-wreck architecture was the stepping-off point for individual developments that were difficult to lump together. Thus we see ex-Mecanoo man Erick van Egeraat emerging with a personal strain of neo-baroque, while his former colleague Francine Houben embarked on a series of sculptural buildings in the second half of the decade.

Very occasionally a trend is so persistent that it becomes a stylistic trait – style after all is the trend of a generation. The best example of a 'fashion style' is dark brick. Since 1994, when the vast Piraeus housing block in Amsterdam by German architect Hans Kollhoff was completed and made a deep impression on Dutch architects, many buildings have been given a dark brick cladding.

Despite the great diversity that followed in the wake of collage architecture, there had been attempts in the years before and after the millennium's end to characterize Dutch architects as a whole. The first and most apposite was 'Reference: OMA', a show mounted in the Netherlands Architecture Institute in Rotterdam in 1995 featuring the work of 16 architects who had worked at Rem Koolhaas's Office for Metropolitan Architecture. The line taken by its curator, the architectural historian Bernard Colenbrander, was that this common past had to have created an affinity between architects like Neutelings Riedijk, Kees Christiaanse, MVRDV and Christian Rapp.

Needless to say, almost all the architects concerned denied having anything in common with the others. Each felt they were too individual to be labelled ex-OMA. That said, Willem Jan Neutelings confirmed that Rem Koolhaas had been at the inception of numerous trends in the Dutch architecture of that time. 'The tilted facade, the urban villa, the contrasting materials, the undulating roofs – a great many trends you see nowadays in middle-of-the-road buildings are OMA ideas of a decade or so ago', said Neutelings in an interview about OMA. More significantly, he acknowledged that the former OMA architects tended to share a 'conceptual approach' to architecture learned from Rem Koolhaas: 'Your analysis of the brief must give you a powerful, unambiguous concept you can use to make your building.'

Winy Maas and Jacob van Rijs of MVRDV in particular proved to be sorceror's apprentices of conceptual architecture. Following Rem Koolhaas's example they were passionate collectors of statistics. And like their teacher, who in 1995 published the doorstep-like *S,M,L,XL* about his work and life, they trotted out a series of ultra-thick books in which analyses of the statistics seemed to lead effortlessly to designs, as if they had replaced the old modernist battle-cry 'form follows function' with 'form follows statistics'.

MVRDV's thickest and most ambitious book, *KM3* (2005), boasts a cool 1,415 pages and is not just about buildings, but also about redesigning regions, countries and even planets. Without exception, the architects of MVRDV follow the same procedure when making a design. First they ask themselves whether, say, Switzerland shouldn't be designed entirely differently to the way it is now. Next, they amass a gigantic quantity of statistics relating to buildings, inhabitants, energy, agriculture, industry and the like. Lastly, their own question is answered with a resounding 'Yes!': of course it could all be done entirely differently. Usually this means that all kinds of facilities and activities now co-existing side by side get stacked, the way the various Dutch landscapes were stacked in the Netherlands Pavilion they designed for the 2000 World Expo in Hanover, Germany.

With their idea that buildings, cities and even entire countries could look utterly different, the work of the three MVRDV architects stands squarely in the modernist tradition. It attests to an anachronistic belief in the idea that society can be the product of social engineering. While politicians and administrators tossed this belief onto the dunghill of history long ago, these architects like many of their early modernist forebears are convinced that their work is capable of improving the world.

The second attempt to assemble Dutch architecture at millennium's end under a single banner was *SuperDutch: New Architecture in the Netherlands*, a book published in 2000 and written by critic Bart Lootsma about 12 'radical' Dutch practices including OMA, Wiel Arets, UNStudio (Ben van Berkel), NOX, Kas Oosterhuis, MVRDV and West 8. Although it was about a heterogeneous group whose work varied from blobs (NOX and Oosterhuis) to 'architecture parlante' (Neutelings Riedijk), Lootsma collectively branded their architecture 'SuperDutch'.

Lootsma linked SuperDutch with the 'second modernity', a concept he adopted from the German Ulrich Beck. The second modernity is that of the digital age and globalization and succeeded the first modernity of the industrial machine age and nationalism. This new modernity is marked by what Lootsma describes as 'global economic and political developments, of the rise of international media networks, and new forms of democracy based on systems of expertise and the political involvement of individual citizens and, not least, of congestion.' With its extremely open economy the Netherlands in his view was particularly sensitive to these developments. It was forced to adapt to the process of globalization more than other countries. This put our trading nation in the forefront of the 'second modernization process'.

In Lootsma's interpretation the forward-looking Dutch consensus-based economy, admired by foreign politicians such as then US president Bill Clinton and British prime minister Tony Blair, single-handedly brought the 'architecture of the second modernity' to full flower.

Hans Ibelings had already given a similar explanation for the emergence of a new type of architecture in his *Supermodernism: Architecture in the Age of Globalization* (1998). Supermodernism, Ibelings wrote, was admittedly not an exclusively Dutch phenomenon, but with buildings by Wiel Arets, Rem Koolhaas, Ben van Berkel and MVRDV it flourished in the Netherlands more than anywhere else in the world.

Supermodernism, Ibelings claimed, was the new international style: 'After postmodernism and its deconstructivist off-shoot, a new architecture now seems to be emerging, an architecture for which such postmodernist notions as place, context and identity have largely lost their meaning.' In the age of instant capital, internet and increasing mobility, he contended, architecture is becoming less and less place-bound. Modernism, which itself was given the name International Style in the US soon after its emergence in the 1920s, had returned in an intensified form and was accordingly dubbed supermodernism by Ibelings. All over the world architects like Rem Koolhaas, Herzog & de Meuron, Dominique Perrault and Toyo Ito were building boxes that from the outside looked even more neutral than the white buildings of concrete, steel and glass of early moderns like Walter Gropius and Mies van der Rohe. They had nothing to do with the surroundings – 'Fuck the context' is one of Koolhaas's most famous statements for good reason. Unconnected to place and time, Ibelings argued, they accorded wonderfully well with the new, digital world in which awareness of time and place was steadily receding.

The case made by Lootsma and Ibelings for the assumed SuperDutch and Supermodernist bearing of Dutch architecture at millennium's end is an echo of the old Marxist reflection theory so popular in the 1970s among sociologists and art historians. According to this theory, changes in the 'material' basis are reflected sooner or later in the 'ideal' superstructure, the province of art and architecture.

But just as the Zeitgeist never dictates anything and always speaks in riddles, the link between material basis and ideal superstructure is seldom clear. For example, the first modernity brought such new building types as the railway station, but generally these were long draped in revival styles such as neogothic. And the Machine Age proceeded in tandem not only with the Modern Movement of the interwar years but equally with a revival of traditionalist and classicist architecture in the 1930s.

The 'second modernity' once again spoke double Dutch in this country, so it transpired at the end of the second millennium. For at the very moment when Ibelings proclaimed that postmodernism was dead and signalled the rise of supermodernism, the Netherlands was overrun by architecture that was unabashedly postmodernist. One example is the large, neo-traditionalist complex of offices, shops and housing built in Groningen in 1996. Its designer was the Italian Adolfo Natalini, a former avant-gardist who had converted to postmodernism in the 1980s. Around 1998, The Hague's Centraal Station found itself in the company of De Resident, a neo-traditionalist urban project of narrow streets and enclosed courts. Built to an urban design by the Luxembourger Rob Krier, the project was filled with buildings by foreign and Dutch postmodernists like Michael Graves, Natalini and Sjoerd Soeters. Even Rotterdam, the capital of Dutch modernism, gained a postmodernist shopping centre near the 1950s Lijnbaan shopping street in the shape of a sunken Italian town. Dubbed 'koopgoot' (spendthrift gully) by the locals, it was designed jointly by Pi de Bruijn and Jon Jerde, an American architect whose fame rested in part on a number of exuberant theme casinos in Las Vegas.

The late breakthrough of postmodernism in this country was not only because, as the cliché goes, everything happens first in the rest of the world and then in the Netherlands. Of greater significance is a phenomenon that also explains the emergence of supermodernism, namely globalization. Globalization has a Janus head, a feature expressed in architecture as supermodernism and postmodernism. Supermodernist architects bow unreservedly to the digital age and the 'second modernity'. Like a surfer on the waves (to quote Rem Koolhaas) they go with the flow of digitization, increasing mobility and the rest and design fuck-context buildings that bear no relation to place and time. But contrary to what Ibelings and other critics averred, globalization does not render concepts like place, context and identity meaningless. On the contrary, globalization, whose context-free architecture is to make the world look the same everywhere, causes many to cry out for their own recognizable place. Those who spend much of their lives at the computer and ride the digital and material highways in virtually identical vehicles have no wish to spend their leisure time in an utterly neutral environment. Many such digital, hypermobile people long for buildings that respond to 'context', provide a 'place' and thereby create a unique 'identity'.

IJ Tower Amsterdam

Neutelings Riedijk Architects 1998

Willem Jan Neutelings and Michiel Riedijk are the pioneers of Dutch neo-expressionism. Their IJ Tower in Amsterdam's eastern docks area, which fell into disuse in the 1960s and 1970s, shows how you can make a sculptural building with the simplest of means. A few deftly placed incisions are enough to liven up what otherwise would be just another prism.
In this building the decoration is, as yet, limited to the strips of the cladding. These modernist decorations recall the I-beams that Ludwig Mies van der Rohe (the less-is-more man) mounted on the frontage of his post-war buildings of steel and glass. But it was not long after the Amsterdam tower block was on site that Neutelings and Riedijk moved on to ever more exuberant decoration, now becoming the pioneers of the 'new decorativeness' in Dutch architecture.

Piraeus Amsterdam

Hans Kollhoff and Christian Rapp 1994

According to the German architects, their Piraeus building in Amsterdam's eastern docks area was inspired by the architecture of the Amsterdam School. That may well be, but the superblock is more closely allied to the German brick expressionism of, say, the Hamburg architect Fritz Höger.
Whatever the case, Piraeus was the most influential building in the Netherlands in the closing decade of the twentieth century. Its sculptural form and the use of dark brick cladding were widely imitated by Dutch architects even after the year 2000.

Schouwburgplein

Rotterdam

Adriaan Geuze/West 8 1997

Adriaan Geuze is one of the Dutch landscape architects to venture into urban design and architecture in the 1990s, blurring the dividing lines between the disciplines. Schouwburgplein is a neo-modernist collage. This all but empty theatre square is in the modernist tradition of open space. Its surface, which has been slightly elevated to form a kind of stage, boasts a wide variety of materials including rubber, epoxy, wood and steel. Seen from the air the square is an abstract geometric composition in the manner of Piet Mondrian. Visitors standing in it mostly see an expanse of grey. Geuze wants to design squares and plazas that can be 'colonized' by those using them. However, bubbles in the rubber, warps in the wood and tears in the metal mean that Schouwburgplein is restricted in its use and therefore difficult to colonize.

de Doelen

Erasmus Bridge

Rotterdam

Van Berkel & Bos architectuurbureau 1996

In the early 1990s the City of Rotterdam was willing to pay an additional 30 million guilders (16,500,000 USD) to ensure landmark status for the Erasmus Bridge, which was to connect the city centre with Zuid (Rotterdam south of the river) – this was before the term 'icon' for striking buildings gained currency in architecture.

Ben van Berkel's 'Erasmusbrug' is allied to the bridges designed by the Spanish architect Santiago Calatrava, who didn't opt for the most logical or economical constructions as an engineer would do. The Erasmus Bridge is a huge success: over the years the cross-river connection to Rotterdam-Zuid has grown into Rotterdam's number one symbol.

Borneo-Sporenburg Amsterdam

Adriaan Geuze/West 8 1996

After Schouwburgplein and other Rotterdam squares, odes to the void, landscape architect Adriaan Geuze presented a tribute to density with his urban master plan for Borneo-Sporenburg. Geuze drew his inspiration for the housing on the two elongated, disused peninsulas of Borneo and Sporenburg from the Jordaan, the densely populated quarter just outside Amsterdam's canal zone. 'Low rise in high density' was the slogan informing Borneo-Sporenburg.
From this stepping-off point came narrow row houses set back to back. Designed by the cream of the architectural world, these had to do without gardens but all have a patio and/or roof terrace. Often 'patio' is stretching it a bit: many houses have one no bigger than a light court like the ones traditional Amsterdam canal houses have between their front and back halves. It took a number of 'superblocks' of apartments, dispersed among the row houses, to achieve the desired high density of 80 units per hectare on Borneo-Sporenburg.

Lensvelt Company Building Breda

Wiel Arets 1999

No phenomenon during the building boom of the past quarter century has been the target of so many complaints as the 'business park'. Not that these had the slightest effect, since the ugliness of these places had an iron logic: everyone involved benefitted from business parks in that form. City councils made a fortune from allocating building plots, builders did equally well from erecting the offices and service buildings, companies got the free-standing building they wanted surrounded by a capacious car park and architects had plenty of work. Now and again the logic of ugliness was countered, for example by the Lensvelt building designed by Wiel Arets. It did mean having a client with ideals, one who had long financed an award for interior design.

Netherlands Pavilion at the World Expo Hanover (DE)

MVRDV 2000

Following the example set by Rem Koolhaas, MVRDV have published a string of ultra-thick books over the years, including *FARMAX* (1998) and *KM3* (2005). These saw the firm's three architects putting the world to rights and, in *KM3* even the universe. Often their solution for organizing the world more efficiently was to stack spaces for activities of all kinds. They caused a sensation with their (unrealized) design for a Pig City, which stacks the many pig farms in this country into skyscrapers.
Just how the Netherlands could be organized differently was expressed by MVRDV in the Netherlands Pavilion for the World Expo in Hanover, Germany in 2000. This took typical Dutch landscapes such as tulip fields and a wood and stacked them, topping off the whole with wind turbines.
Expo 2000 was all about sustainability and the participating countries were requested to erect their pavilion in materials that could be recycled. This is not what happened with the Dutch pavilion. It still stands in the Expo grounds where it has degenerated into an impressive ruin complete with dead trees.

Educatorium Utrecht

OMA/Rem Koolhaas 1997

The Educatorium, a building containing lecture halls and a student restaurant, stands in De Uithof, the campus area of Utrecht University on the city's eastern rim. Masterplanned by Art Zaaijer and OMA, this is where the university has assembled, over the years, a galaxy of educational buildings by Dutch architects including Neutelings Riedijk, Mecanoo, Marlies Rohmer and Herman Hertzberger. So De Uithof can be considered an open-air museum of contemporary Dutch architecture.

The most remarkable component of Rem Koolhaas's Educatorium is the concrete fold. This feature was in vogue in the years around 1997. MVRDV's Villa VPRO is another to have one.

Koolhaas was a pioneer of the fashion for folds. His never realized designs for Zentrum für Kunst und Medientechnologie Karlsruhe (1990) and the Jussieu libraries in Paris (1992) already include folded floor planes. There is a famous photograph taken at OMA's office which shows how a building of folded floors can be made by making a few cuts in a single sheet of paper.

De Resident The Hague

Rob Krier completed 2011

De Resident is an urban renewal project near The Hague Centraal Station. In the 1960s, this part of town had already been altered drastically with the arrival of a batch of modernist ministry buildings and 30 years later it underwent a second transformation courtesy of a design by the Luxembourg postmodernist Rob Krier. On the site of those stand-alone ministry buildings Krier projected what he calls a 'European city', that is, an area of enclosed squares and narrow streets hemmed in by the march of mute facades.
Architects from home and abroad, amongst whom the Italian Adolfo Natalini, the Argentine American Cesar Pelli and Dutch representatives Sjoerd Soeters and Karelse Van der Meer (now De Zwarte Hond), were invited to design the buildings. Krier himself took on one tower block (Muzentoren).
The brief for Disney architect Michael Graves to convert a modernist office building into a 'Dutch' building with a brick facade, vertical windows and two enormous gable roofs – known locally as 'the pair of tits' – precipitated a minor riot. Carel Weeber, chairman of the Union of Dutch Architects or BNA, protested noisily against granting such a prestigious commission in the political heart of the Netherlands to a foreigner.

Muzenplein

Almere City Centre

Rem Koolhaas/OMA c. 2005

For more than 20 years, the most attractive part of the new polder town of Almere was an empty expanse on the shore of the artificial lake of Weerwater (Water again). It was only at the beginning of the 1990s that OMA was commissioned to draw up a master plan for the area, in which shops, housing and cultural buildings (cinema, theatre, library etcetera) were to make it the vibrant centre of Almere.
Although OMA is the flagship of SuperDutch architecture, the master plan for Almere city centre marks a return to medieval town planning. It sites a thick wad of buildings atop a parking facility and a bus lane. Out of this wad, which rises towards its centre as a low hill, the streets and squares have been incised as in old, densely built-up European towns. Surprisingly, this strategy makes the new centre of Almere an extremely close relative of De Resident in The Hague, for which Rob Krier had made a similarly 'old European' plan.
Big names from home and abroad were brought in to design the buildings. The Englishman William Alsop designed a hotel and a blob-shaped pop/rock venue, the Frenchman Christian de Portzamparc row houses above shops and Japanese Pritzker Prize winners SANAA a theatre in the lake.
Of the Dutch contingent, Meyer en Van Schooten designed the library, Claus en Kaan and René van Zuuk were assigned apartment buildings and OMA itself took on the cinema.

SHOP ONLINE
WE
FASHION.
COM

Brandevoort Helmond

Rob Krier 1996

At about the same time that De Resident was taking shape in The Hague, work began on another Rob Krier master plan: that for Brandevoort, Helmond's Vinex housing development. Brandevoort was nothing like the other new housing estates at the turn of the millennium. Krier designed it as a traditional town the North Brabant province, its centre containing canals and surrounded by a 'moat', as if Brandevoort had once been a fortified town. The canal houses, designed by a number of Dutch architects, exhibit a great variety in their frontage and roof heights, giving the impression that each has been commissioned and built privately. Brandevoort was a huge success. It allowed Krier to design a score of new housing developments in the Netherlands, whether or not in the form of fortified towns. It also saw his postmodernist urbanism taken up by many Dutch architects. Even the SuperDutch firm of West 8 designed a canal town. This made Krier the most influential architect in the Netherlands of the early twenty-first century.

Fuck the Zeitgeist

Chapter 5

Until the end of the 1990s postmodernism was largely an import product in the Netherlands. In the 1980s, for example, a residents' association invited the Belgian architect Charles Vandenhove to The Hague to redesign parts of its nineteenth-century areas along neoclassicist lines. Vandenhove's urban renewal, complete with courtyard housing or *hofjes*, was a triumph: large ensembles in Amsterdam, Maastricht, Breda and other cities would follow.

It was the wayward loners among Dutch architects who made sporadic forays into postmodern architecture. In 1990, three years after the Netherlands' sole glamour architect Cees Dam gave the Options Exchange on Amsterdam's Rokin the look of a Renaissance palazzo, an unabashedly postmodern stockbroker's office took its place in the same street. It earned its architect, Mart van Schijndel, the derision of his Dutch colleagues in particular who considered his blatant postmodernism to be un-Dutch. And they were partly right. Even though the Netherlands would later prove to be fertile ground for postmodernism, the underlying concept has never found its way into Dutch architectural discourse. The work of Rob Krier, the Luxembourg architect who built a variation on the fortified towns theme at various places in the Netherlands, has never been described by the majority of Dutch critics as postmodernist or postmodern, but instead as 'historicist' or, more often, 'retro'. Particularly that last qualification is almost always used in a negative sense. Which is why architectural historian Hans Ibelings gave his 2004 paperback on Dutch postmodernist architecture the neutral title *Unmodern Architecture*. In the subtitle he uses another term for it: 'Contemporary Traditionalism in the Netherlands'.

Later, in 2010, Ibelings and fellow architectural historian Vincent van Rossem together wrote *The New Tradition*. This concept seems the same as neo-traditionalism, the most significant postmodernist style in the Netherlands. But several of their colleagues, among whom Bernard Colenbrander, had objections to the term neo-traditionalism. Much of the work described as neo-traditionalist, he felt, bore little if any resemblance to the serious, twentieth-century traditionalism of architects like Granpré Molière and Berghoef.

But whether we call it retro, anti-modern, unmodern, historicist, new traditional or neo-traditionalist, postmodernism has continued to enjoy an unparalleled success in this country. It wasn't Rem Koolhaas and his Office for Metropolitan Architecture who led the field of influential architects in the Netherlands at the start of the twenty-first century but the fiercely anti-modernist Luxembourger Rob Krier. After the success of Brandevoort, Krier's Vinex housing development in Helmond based on a traditional fortified town, many Dutch architects were quick to jump on the postmodernist bandwagon.

But no matter how widespread postmodernism in the Netherlands has become, it still manages to evoke moral outrage. In 2010, for example, the then BNA chairman Bjarne Mastenbroek, possessed of an unshakeable faith in the spirit of the times as some Dutch architects still are, described neo-traditionalism in a letter to the editor in *NRC Handelsblad* as 'this country's best sold lie'. He compared neo-traditionalist architects with populist politicians like Rita Verdonk and Geert Wilders: 'Their main strength is in shouting their mouths off about some problem or other without knowing the first thing about it, let alone suggesting a decent solution.'

A few months later, the designer-critic Ronald Hooft in a review in the Dutch daily *Het Parool* made the connection between populism and neo-traditionalism. Although he awarded De Meander (2001), a large residential block by Rob Krier in Amsterdam's Staatslieden area of predominantly social housing, four stars out of five, he ended his review with the remark that many of its residents undoubtedly voted for Geert Wilders' right-wing Party for Freedom (PVV).

Even the timid postmodernist Jo Coenen condemned Krier's Brandevoort in a documentary in 2006, labelling the project 'artificial' and 'false'. And falsehoods did not go unnoticed by the god of architecture, he added threateningly, sounding like an orthodox protestant minister. Four years earlier, critic Bart Lootsma, the author of *SuperDutch,* in a German lecture described the one colleague who had not spoken disparagingly about the rise of neo-traditionalism as an exponent of *Volksempfinden,* 'popular instinct'. *Volksempfinden,* as all Lootsma's German listeners were aware, was invariably accompanied by the word *gesund* ('sound') and the most fervent advocates of the *gesunde Volksempfinden,* the 'sound popular instinct', as even non-Germans are aware, were the adherents of National Socialism, the political movement with which Wilders' Party for Freedom has been regularly compared.

This connection between neo-traditionalism and populism is as general as it is misleading. Neo-traditionalism, after all, made its entrance in Dutch architecture back in the early 1990s, a full decade before populist politicians like Pim Fortuyn attracted a major following. So the late breakthrough of postmodernism didn't mean that the Netherlands had become a country of populist architecture but that it had begun to draw level with the rest of the Western world. Just as in, say, France and Germany, the Netherlands now at last enjoyed a wide diversity of styles, from neo-modernist to neo-traditionalist and everything in between.

It is because of the moralism in Dutch architecture that there has never been a productive debate about neo-traditionalism. Architecture remained a question of right and wrong, and of belief, as Sjoerd Soeters stated in an interview in 2006. 'It's all down to a very simple belief', he explained. 'Innovation is right, tradition is wrong. It's incredibly Calvinist, as if there were an assembly of finger-wagging clergy that excommunicates anyone who thinks differently.'

This led to the paradox that although most Dutch architects regard 'style' as an outdated notion, Dutch architecture is still largely a question of form. 'Sticking with Calvinist terminology', Soeters continued, 'it's really just about whether or not you wear a black suit. If you do what MVRDV has done and parachute a bright orange box into the courtyard of an old housing block, which has all the locals up in arms, then you get one article after another in the professional press and you're sure to end up in the *Architecture Yearbook*. If you design a pleasant neighbourhood of soothing brick houses, you needn't expect a write-up in the magazines. And this when in my mind it's the second of these that matters: how to make comfortable architecture where most people feel at home.'

To illustrate the standard of Dutch architectural discourse, Soeters went on to describe a bus trip he had organized for architects and designers to Haverleij, the Vinex housing development his firm had designed on the River Maas outside Den Bosch. Haverleij deviates from all the other Vinex developments in that instead of being spread across the site as low-rise, the housing is concentrated in nine castle-like apartment buildings and one fortified town by the ubiquitous Rob Krier. Open green areas extend between the castles: 'The new government architect Mels Crouwel had said in an interview that he thought the back-to-the-classics side of my work was godawful. I then rang him up and asked whether he and the other government advisors on landscape and infrastructure would pay Haverleij a visit, just to see for themselves. On arriving, one of the advisors initially refused to get out of the bus. Seems he didn't want to see Haverleij in the flesh. But after a while he must have got bored sitting there by himself and sulkily joined the rest of the group.'

But even though Dutch moralism has more of a religious than a political face, the success of neo-traditionalism in the Netherlands ultimately does have a political basis. The breakthrough of postmodernism is the direct consequence of the biggest political upheaval in Dutch housing construction since the National Housing Act of 1901, namely when housing associations were given financial independence in 1995. In that year central government wrote off the debts of the housing associations in exchange for the termination of subsidies and preferential loans. From then on, the corporations were on their own and had to take care of their revenues and loans themselves. This brought about a seismic shift in the world of Dutch domestic construction. Since becoming independent it is no longer the housing associations that account for the lion's share of housing in this country but property developers and large construction firms, whether or not in association with local government in public-private partnerships.

This independence accorded the housing associations did not mean the end of the celebrated Dutch social housing, as is sometimes claimed. About 30 per cent of new build housing in the urban restructuring areas and Vinex developments still consists today of social rented units. On the other hand, housing has become more commercial since 1994. Property developers are taking greater note, out of market considerations, of the wishes of home buyers than the corporations, which for decades had built subsidized rented units in a tight housing market. Home buyers, as property developers know from the findings of lifestyle research, often have a preference for traditional architecture. And they're willing to pay more for it, according to a study carried out by the Netherlands Environmental Assessment Agency (PBL) in 2014: neo-traditionalist new build houses were 14 per cent more expensive than 'regular' houses at the start of the twenty-first century.

A new stage in Dutch postmodernism emerged after 2005: firms like FARO Architects, Heren 5 and De Zwarte Hond, who until then had shown not the slightest interest in neo-traditionalism, began adopting its stylistic traits. Even West 8, Adriaan Geuze's office for landscape architecture which as late as 2000 could still be called SuperDutch, went on to design the neo-traditionalist neighbourhood De Laak in Vathorst, the Amersfoort Vinex development. With its canals and dark brick-clad canal houses De Laak is a dead ringer for Krier's Brandevoort. With one difference – the Amersfoort canal houses, designed by De Zwarte Hond and others, are tauter and more restrained than those in Brandevoort. Jurgen van der Ploeg of FARO Architects coined the oxymoron 'contemporary retro' to describe this style.

'Contemporary retro' brings to mind the brick classicism of Dutch architects like Abraham van der Hart (1747–1820) or the German Biedermeier architecture of around 1800, styles regarded by some architectural historians as distant precursors of modernism because of their restraint and sparing use of decoration. Its proto-modernist character made Dutch classicism an acceptable style for former adherents of schoolteachers' modernism such as the architects of FARO. But their predilection for 'contemporary retro' does have a downside: 15 years after the breakthrough of postmodernism much neo-traditionalist architecture in the Netherlands looks the same. It is as if a recipe had been found for contemporary retro: take some taut, unadorned facades in dark brick, top these off with pitched black-tiled roofs and add a little light variation, say with the odd recess and by rotating the roofs, so that it seems as if the houses were not all erected at once by the same property developer but, just as at the turn of the eighteenth and nineteenth centuries, individually commissioned and built.

Thus, this preference among architects for contemporary retro in the early twenty-first century Netherlands gave rise to the paradox that the postmodernist efforts to achieve individuality resulted in uniformity. Modern traditionalist buildings look so much alike these days that from their appearance you could just as easily be in a neighbourhood designed by Scala and Mulleners + Mulleners in the Schuytgraaf Vinex development in Arnhem as in a new housing estate by West 8 in Loenen aan de Vecht.

Several explanations have been put forward for the new uniformity in Dutch architecture. Sjoerd Soeters attributed the success of neo-traditionalism to the fact that the Dutch like a bandwagon to leap on. 'Here in the Netherlands we have this remarkable combination of high consensus and sudden about-turns in public opinion', said Soeters in an interview in 2006: 'The American historian James Kennedy a few years back referred to this phenomenon in connection with the Dutch attitude to minority ethnic groups. To begin with, the general attitude was that nothing disparaging should be said about ethnic minorities yet after Pim Fortuyn they were more reviled here than anywhere else in Europe. It's the same with neo-traditionalism. First it was taboo in this country but now clients hardly want anything else.'

Soeters also concludes that Dutch neo-traditionalism is to a large extent superficial: 'Many neo-traditionalist buildings get built without due consideration. The fact that many houses are built in dark brick we owe to the German architect Hans Kollhoff and his Piraeus building in Amsterdam. This dark building from 1994 made a huge impression on Dutch architects. And so now you see very many architects designing buildings with dark brick cladding and deeply recessed windows as if they were old converted factories. Very gloomy all round, when the Dutch building tradition is one of bricks in all colours, many of them light. And the windows in many old houses have attractive white frames and even white surrounds. They are more than just a gap in the wall, they are the eyelids, the eyelashes of a building.'

According to the German architectural sociologist Werner Sewing, who in 2005 signed for the Premsela Lecture in the Beurs van Berlage in Amsterdam, contemporary retro is an international phenomenon: neo-traditionalist architects throughout the Western world have a predilection for the style at the end of the eighteenth century. 'It's impossible to return to the Middle Ages', he said in an interview: 'And the Renaissance is of little use to us, as it's too distant as well. But the period around 1800, the age of Biedermeier in Germany and brick classicism in the Netherlands, is able to speak to us. It is the age of *Gemütlichkeit*, a state so desired these days, a life of comfort and contentment. If we can believe Paul Mebes and Paul Emmerich, two architects who published the book *Um 1800* (Circa 1800) a century ago, it was also the last period in which craftsmanship enjoyed a high standard. After 1800, they felt, industrialization sent traditional building construction into a decline.'

Besides, Biedermeier and Dutch neoclassicism have modernist traits, Sewing added: 'Both styles have minimalist sides. This may explain their attraction for current neo-traditionalist architects who often began their career as modernists.'

Stationsstraat

The Hague

Charles Vandenhove 1987

Rob Krier's success in the 1990s was preceded by that of the Belgian postmodernist Charles Vandenhove. In the 1980s Vandenhove was invited by residents of the Schilderswijk area in The Hague to design housing blocks as part of the urban renewal programme. This accomplished, Vandenhove went on to assemble a comprehensive body of work in the Netherlands – more than he would build in his own country. Not just in The Hague but in Amsterdam, Breda, Maastricht and many other cities, his housing blocks are in a style that recalls Haussmann's Paris of the nineteenth century yet is unmistakably that of Vandenhove. At the end of the 1990s, Vandenhove designed law courts for Shyam Khandekar's master plan for Paleiskwartier near the station in Den Bosch.
Unlike Krier's work later, that of Charles Vandenhove in 1985–1995 was not emulated by other architects. The housing associations had not yet become independent and many Dutch architects were at that time in thrall to schoolteachers' modernism.

Reconstruction of Waagstraat

Groningen

Adolfo Natalini 1996

Jo Vegter's post-war extension to the town hall on Waagstreet in Groningen was demolished to build this retail and housing complex, a project that marked the breakthrough of postmodernism in the Netherlands. Natalini was one of six architects competing to design the ensemble. In a referendum about the entries, which the city council declared to be binding, the vast majority of townsfolk expressed their preference for Natalini's olde-worlde design, to the consternation of the competition jury. The story goes that when selecting architects for the competition Groningen's spatial planning department had assumed that Natalini, founder of the celebrated Superstudio, had always been an avant-gardist and was unaware that the Italian had since been converted to postmodernism.

Bonnefanten-museum Maastricht

Aldo Rossi 1995

The Italian architect Aldo Rossi (1931–1997), one of the 'Rats' in Aldo van Eyck's infamous lecture 'Rats, Posts and Other Pests' (1981), was known in the 1960s as a pioneer of neo-rationalism. The name of this trend suggests that it signified a revival of *razionalismo*, the Italian version of modernism from the Mussolini era, with Giuseppe Terragni its best-known representative. And looking at Rossi's housing block (1971) in the Gallatarese area of Milan, this was indeed originally the case. Architecturally at all events, since Rossi the urban designer was a post-modernist from day one. His principal theoretical work, *L'Architettura della città* (1966), is an argument against the modernist urbanism of 'light, air and space' and for the traditional, densely built-up city.

In his later architecture Rossi often referred to traditional architecture and to archetypes. His urban villa on Berlin's Rauchstrasse, for example, his contribution to the International Architecture Exhibition (IBA) in the early 1980s, is a throw-back to that city's factory architecture and tenement buildings of the nineteenth century. Rossi's Bonnefantenmuseum in Maastricht, built at a time when postmodernism in the Netherlands was largely an import product, makes similar reference with its brick external walls and steel beams to old factory architecture – the museum occupies the site of a former factory. But it is also a variation on the classic nineteenth century museum, being a symmetrical building with two wings and an enfilade of rooms off a central area with a grand staircase. As if to catch the attention Rossi added to this classic ensemble a zinc-clad tower resembling the archetypal space rocket in the Georges Méliès film *A Trip to the Moon* (1902).

Ruin Housing Amersfoort

Leo Heijdenrijk 1991

Kattenbroek, the Amersfoort housing development built at the time when the Supplement to the Fourth National Policy Document on Physical Planning (Vinex) was being drawn up, is the mother of all Vinex settlements. Its post-modernist design, by urban planner Ashok Bhalotra at the end of the 1980s, would be widely imitated in the 100-plus Vinex developments built throughout the Netherlands after 1995.

Bhalotra gave Kattenbroek a structure that recalls a capricious geometric-abstract painting from the early 1920s by Russian artist Wassily Kandinsky. The different parts of Kattenbroek were allotted themes like 'The Hidden Zone' and 'The Mask'. The architecture of its housing was similarly diverse. At times this too was unabashedly postmodernist, then very much the exception in this country. One example is Leo Heijdenrijk's ruin housing: row houses with crumbling brick facades.

The initial reactions to Kattenbroek by most critics and fellow architects were brusque and disparaging. They regarded Bhalotra as an Indian cloud-dweller and the mysterious themes as self-indulgently sentimental. Most of all, they felt that postmodern architecture was out of place in the Netherlands. That said, Kattenbroek was a great success with the public at large and among councillors and property developers. As a result, many Dutch designers went on to design similarly themed suburbs in the age of Vinex.

Circus Zandvoort

Sjoerd Soeters 1991

Circus, which combines a cinema and an amusement hall cum fruit machine arcade in the seaside resort of Zandvoort, is the Netherlands' first undiluted Las Vegas building. Sjoerd Soeters made it a bona fide 'duck', as postmodernism's principal theorists, Robert Venturi and Denise Scott Brown, call a building that expresses what it is: Circus looks like a circus (although funnily enough it isn't one). The roofs are shaped like the peaks of tents and flags frozen in mid-flutter clamour for the attention of passers-by. Soeters is the only Dutch architect not to complain about being labelled a postmodernist. This earned him a reputation as the bad boy of Dutch architecture but has done nothing to hamper his progress. In the past decade Soeters has emerged as an urban designer who is able to transform desolate parts of town into pleasant areas with traditional squares and streets. His is an extensive body of work that has enjoyed remarkable success among critics in recent years.

Stockbroker's Office Amsterdam

Mart van Schijndel 1990

Mart van Schijndel's stockbroker's office on Amsterdam's Rokin is one of the earlier examples of undiluted postmodernism in Dutch architecture. Like the canal houses either side of it – Rokin used to be a canal – the office has a classical composition. Perhaps it is even a little too ostentatiously classical. The striped facade, the pediment and the glitzy mirror-glass of the windows and bay give the feeling that Van Schijndel's construction-kit classicism is intended as a parody of post-modernism. It is as if the architect wants to say: 'Look, that's how easy it is to make a postmodern building!'
And yet the Stockbroker's Office is meant to be taken seriously. It was no isolated incident in Van Schijndel's work. He often gave a classical touch to buildings he designed for old city centres, such as the apartments from 1995 on Pieterskerkhof, a street and square in Utrecht.

De Laak Amersfoort

West 8 2005

One way to upset the designers of West 8 is to tell them that their design for De Laak, a neighbourhood in Vathorst, Amersfoort's Vinex development, clearly betrays the influence of Brandevoort, Rob Krier's Vinex settlement disguised as a fortified town. The former SuperDutch architects deny any influence from Krier's direction. And yet there are unmistakable similarities between De Laak and Brandevoort. Not only does De Laak have canals, one of which is a dead ringer for the 'moat' in Brandevoort, but the canal houses in De Laak also seem commissioned and built individually.
Of course there are differences too. If the canal houses in Brandevoort seek to really look old, the ones in De Laak are 'contemporary retro': they are tauter and less modulated. Besides, here and there between the modern retro in De Laak are houses whose flat roofs and copper and glass fronts endow them with explicitly 'contemporary' aspirations.

Floriande Eiland 2

Hoofddorp

Mulleners + Mulleners architecten and Nowotny architecten 2004

A strategy often used in Vinex developments to give neighbourhoods a degree of seclusion is to divide them up into islands. For Eiland 2, one of the 12 islands comprising Floriande, Hoofddorp's Vinex settlement, Mulleners + Mulleners have based their urban master plan on a fortified town. Three sides of the island consist of green strips with trees and pathways, as if there used to be ramparts here. The island also has car-free narrow streets and small squares.
For the housing the architects adopted a no-frills traditionalism allied to the Biedermeier style of around 1800. It is to this style that many neo-traditionalist architects turn, and not just in this country.

Leliënhuyze Den Bosch

Soeters Van Eldonk architecten 2005

Of all the castles built in Haverleij until now, the one by Sjoerd Soeters is the most castle-like. Soeters, who decided that the Vinex settlement should consist of a compact fortified town and nine 'castles' of apartments, added corner towers and jutting bays to Leliënhuyze. He also inserted large stone arches in the brick frontage, as if they had had a long and eventful life.
Haverleij is the most unusual of all the Vinex projects. It marks a radical break with the Dutch tradition of rolling out each new residential development carpet-like across the landscape. By concentrating the buildings in a 'town' and nine 'castles', there was room left in between for a park and a golf course to a design by Paul van Beek. In addition, part of the existing polder landscape along the River Maas was retained. This experiment did entail that Haverleij with five housing units per hectare has a much lower development density than the average Vinex settlement of 25 units per hectare. The castles of Haverleij were declared the first gated community in the Netherlands. Incorrectly, as it happens, as the castle courtyards have been freely accessible since day one.

De Bras The Hague

FARO Architects and Heren 5

2009

Old Dutch villages and Mondrian's *New York Boogie Woogie* were the twin sources of inspiration for De Bras, a neighbourhood in Ypenburg whose urban design and architecture were both the work of FARO Architects and Heren 5. The 'directed anarchy', as the architects describe their design, has produced a residential area that breaks with the tradition of Dutch row houses in serried ranks. Fluctuating building lines, asymmetrical street channels and drainage ditches crossed by bridges inject a rustic, informal ambience. That said, with 37 units per hectare the development density here is higher than is customary in Dutch suburbs with long rows of terraced housing. To add an element of unity, all houses have roofs pitched at an angle of 53 degrees, an angle usually come across in traditional Dutch farmhouses.

Op Buuren Stichtse Vecht

La4Sale and Mulleners + Mulleners architecten 2014

Just as Krier's Brandevoort was to be a traditional Brabant village, so Op Buuren, a new residential neighbourhood in Stichtse Vecht, north of Utrecht, is intended as a 'village on the Vecht' (the river running through that municipality). To achieve this its designers adopted a working method similar to that used by OMA/Rem Koolhaas when designing IJplein in 1980. They distilled their twenty-first century village not from existing modernist plans but from old towns and villages along the Vecht such as Muiden, Weesp and Breukelen. Op Buuren, built on a cleaned-up industrial estate, consists of three parts: Op Buuren Park, Op Buuren Buiten (inspired by the seventeenth-century country houses or *buitenhuizen* along the Vecht) and Op Buuren Dorp (village). A newly dug canal stitches it all together. Eight architects designed the canal houses and apartment buildings. The lion's share is in a neo-traditionalist style. But 'to reflect the spirit of the times', as the neighbourhood's developers Kondor Wessels and Bouwfonds put it, it has the occasional neo-modernist box by Liesbeth van der Pol, amongst others.

Vögele

Glass Farm Schijndel

MVRDV 2012

The world's thinnest farmhouse, with architecture a mere two millimetres thick, is how Winy Maas of MVRDV describes the glass building in the guise of a Brabant farmhouse on the church square in Schijndel, the village where he was born. The exterior walls and roof of the building, which houses shops, a café and a wellness centre, consist of glass panels onto which details of all the still existing local farms have been printed.

The Glass Farm is bona fide conceptual architecture. A committee drawn from Schijndel's municipal council determined the volume this building was to occupy on Schijndel's central square. The volume in question 'cried out to be a farmhouse', according to Maas. 'And this was to be made of traditional materials like brick and wood. And glass . . .' MVRDV's Glass Farm is their riposte to retro architecture, which Maas regards as anachronistic and therefore inappropriate. The trumped-up farmhouse has something of a parody, or even a joke. But Maas insists it's a serious design: 'A joke? I wouldn't dare. My parents still live in Schijndel.'

Inverdan Zaanstad

Soeters Van Eldonk architecten 2013

Grozny after a Russian bombing raid, is how Sjoerd Soeters described the centre of Zaanstad, northwest of Amsterdam, at the onset of the twenty-first century. Soeters changed this with Inverdan, the official name of the urban renewal project for the central area around Zaanstad railway station. The development (shops, a cinema, a new city hall, a hotel and a great many apartments) is dense and cut through by a newly dug narrow canal flanked by walkways. An elevated cycle- and footpath leads across the provincial road, long a physical barrier in Zaanstad, to skirt and access the station, alongside which is now the entrance, on an elevated plaza, to the city hall. If the urban design of Inverdan is postmodernist, various buildings in the new centre of Zaanstad are candidates for what we can call super-postmodernist. The city hall, designed by Soeters himself, consists of not one but four 'decorated sheds', as Robert Venturi and Denise Scott Brown called simple boxes with an embellished facade in the postmodernist bible *Learning from Las Vegas* (1972). The neighbouring Inntel Hotel, designed by WAM architecten, with its facade of stacked local wooden houses, has been called a 'decorated duck', a combination of 'decorated shed' and 'duck', Venturi and Scott Brown's term for 'architecture parlante'.

(Con)fusion

Chapter 6

Just how eloquently the Zeitgeist speaks double Dutch and how undefined and confusing the connection between architecture and populism really is, could be gauged from the debate on the building of mosques in the 2000s. This began in the autumn of 2003, just before the foundation stone of the Essalam Mosque in Rotterdam was to be laid. It all revolved around the question that the nineteenth-century architect Heinrich Hübsch had tried to answer back in 1828 in his book *In welchem Style sollen wir bauen*, in what style should we build?

The Essalam Mosque, a design by Molenaar & Van Winden based on nineteenth-century Mamluk architecture from Cairo and the twentieth-century Jumeirah Mosque in Dubai, was to be a mosque with a dome and two minarets. Marco Pastors, then a Rotterdam alderman and leader of the populist political party Leefbaar Rotterdam (liveable Rotterdam), felt that this was two minarets and a dome too many. 'The design is a misleading signal, a reference to the past', he said of the Essalam Mosque in *de Volkskrant* daily paper in 2003: 'This is something you only find in provincial areas of Islamic countries. The mosques in Toronto and Rio de Janeiro are more modern; open, forward-looking. This is want we should have – a signal that we want to advance and that we're working on integration.'

Pastors would have got what he wanted from Ergün Erkoçu and Abdeluahab Hammiche, two architecture students who had joined forces as MEMAR (Turkish for architect) and whose graduation project was an alternative for the Essalam Mosque. 'Polder mosque' is what the two Dutchmen of Turkish and Moroccan descent respectively called their neo-modernist design for a mosque without minarets but with something resembling a dome. To be built of steel and concrete and masses of glass, MEMAR's never realized mosque bears a strong resemblance to the 1932 design, also never realized, by the Russian Constructivist Moisei Ginzburg for the Palace of the Soviets in Moscow.

'Nostalgia mosques' is how the two MEMAR architects described more or less traditionalist mosques like the Essalam Mosque and another Rotterdam example, Bert Toorman's Mevalana Mosque from 2001. 'They relate to the first generation of Muslim immigrants who still make up the boards of most Dutch mosques', they told *NRC Handelsblad* in 2005: 'Nostalgia mosques are part of the Moroccan identity in Morocco, but not of that in the Netherlands, which is changing fast. We've noticed that our peers have no affinity with domes and minarets. They'd rather have a decent space than an expensive dome.'

Conversely, Molenaar & Van Winden described MEMAR's design as a 'clandestine mosque', after the clandestine, 'hidden' Catholic churches built in this country after Protestantism had become the state religion in the Netherlands at the end of the sixteenth century. The aversion to traditional domed mosques by politicians like Pastors, and later Wilders, they compared to the horror felt by Protestants at the 800 or so mainly neogothic Catholic churches built after the reestablishment of the Episcopal hierarchy in the Netherlands in 1853. Just as the often vast Catholic churches were then an expression of the emancipation of believers in the Catholic faith, so the neo-traditionalist mosques today express the identity of almost one million Islamic immigrants in the Netherlands, they feel. For Molenaar & Van Winden, domed mosques are associated with the multicultural society, which is an established fact and always will be, whether populist politicians like it or not.

Though the two MEMAR partners are themselves confirmed champions of the multicultural society, their polder mosque was embraced by populist politicians who were in fact loudly announcing the demise of that very society. Paradoxically, populism is not aligned with neo-traditionalism in the debate on mosques, but with modernism, the style long associated principally with social democracy, which according to politicians like Wilders is the movement most responsible for the multicultural society.

Despite the political objections the Essalam Mosque did get built in the end, although the process was plagued with difficulties and delays and the mosque even now is still not fully completed. MEMAR's polder mosque remained unbuilt, but the term was hijacked by the former fundamentalist Muslim Mohammed Cheppih. In 2008 he launched in an empty modernist office building in Amsterdam's Nieuw-West area the Polder Mosque, where men and women could pray together unsegregated. Two years later the Amsterdam Polder Mosque folded due to lack of funds.

Even so, the 2000s saw the arrival of several polder mosques *sans* minarets. One of the first to be built (in 2009) was the multifunctional centre designed by Marlies Rohmer in Amsterdam's Transvaal neighbourhood. The building includes two prayer spaces (one for Turkish Muslims, the other for Moroccans) and rooms for training and cultural activities. These are concealed behind a facade which except for a single large expanse of glass consists entirely of brick in a variety of bonds. The exterior refers as much to Arabic decoration as to the Amsterdam School, the architectural style shared by several buildings in the area.

That blending of styles was one reason why Rohmer gave her centre the name 'Fusion'. That word was also used to characterize the style of Le Medi (2009), a 'Mediterranean' housing complex designed by Geurst & Schulze in Rotterdam. Le Medi not only has outdoor spaces that are a cross between old Dutch *hofjes* and Arabic courtyards but also a decorativeness derived from traditional Arabic, Dutch and Byzantine architecture.

Fusion became an official term to denote a style in Dutch architecture when Wilfried van Winden, one half of Molenaar & Van Winden, drew up the 2010 manifesto whose title translates as 'Fusion. An appeal for a decorative architecture'. 'Fusion is the architecture of an open mind that does not accept taboos,' Van Winden writes in his manifesto for an architecture of the multicultural society: 'It's not about razing stylistic boundaries alone but mental ones too. The increasing diversity of cultures requires a new architectural strategy. Fusion stands for an inventive way of mixing and interconnecting present and past, East and West, tradition and innovation, and high and low culture.'

A new departure in Van Winden's architecture without frontiers is that he expressly argues for a fusion between East and West. Apart from that, though, Fusion is little different from the kind of architecture that the father and mother of postmodernism, the American architects Robert Venturi and Denise Scott Brown, were calling for back in 1966 in their book *Complexity and Contradiction in Architecture*. Fusion also recalls the 'double-coding' that British-American architecture critic Charles Jencks, in *The Language of Post-Modern Architecture* (1977), regards as one of the key characteristics of postmodernist architecture: architecture should speak not just to a limited audience of fellow architects but to the general public as well. In this respect, fusion shows above all that postmodernism, twenty years after having been declared dead, is alive and well in the Netherlands.

Essalam Mosque

Rotterdam

Molenaar & Van Winden 2011

This Rotterdam mosque was the subject of fierce debate among politicians and architects. The populist Rotterdam politician Marco Pastors felt that the traditional Essalam Mosque, with its two minarets and a dome, was an expression of the client's failure to integrate, the client being a group of Moroccan Muslims. 'Nostalgia mosque' is how the two young architects of the MEMAR practice described it, a manifestation of the desire for a world that no longer existed. The architects, Joris Molenaar and Wilfried van Winden, regarded their Essalam Mosque instead as proof that the Moroccan Muslims had become emancipated. Just as the emancipating Dutch Catholics built large neogothic churches in the second half of the nineteenth century, so the Muslims were erecting their neo-traditionalist mosques today. For Molenaar and Van Winden, mosques with minarets and domes are inextricably bound up with a Dutch multicultural society of many years' standing.

Islamic Funeral Pavilion

Amsterdam

Furkan Köse/Atelier Puuur 2012

The Islamic funeral pavilion in the south-western corner of the Nieuwe Ooster cemetery in Amsterdam is pure fusion architecture. In this pavilion Furkan Köse has united the Western modernist style with Oriental Islamic architecture. Köse was assisted in this venture as there are very few rules pertaining to an Islamic prayer space. In principle any space can perform this duty. A recess in a wall facing Mecca, the direction Muslims must bow when praying, is handy but even this is not a strict requirement. All the same, most clients are committed to what they regard as the real thing: a building with a dome and minarets. Here Köse has managed to avoid this stereotype. His pavilion is a simple yellow brick clad box. To achieve the necessary orientation to Mecca, the prayer hall has been rotated slightly inside the box, leaving room for a courtyard and other spaces.

De Oriënt The Hague

WAM architecten 2011

ERA Contour, the property developer who commissioned Le Medi, the Dutch-Mediterranean housing complex in Rotterdam, was also responsible for getting De Oriënt built in The Hague. This residential project of 100 housing units in the Transvaal neighbourhood is primarily tailored to the Surinamese-Hindustani population – The Hague has the second biggest Hindustani community in Europe, after London.
The target group could sit on panels to make known their wishes for the project, designed by WAM architecten. Some of these wishes were surprising: it transpired that Hindustani residents were not particularly interested in gardens. A decent, safe place for the car was more important, they felt. Wilfried van Winden designed De Oriënt in the style of the New Hague School of architects with oriental elements added on. Its red brick walls and white bays see De Oriënt responding to the architecture round about. Glazed brick in vivid colours such as purple and yellow and mock-oriental ironwork decorations were to give the project an Eastern ambience. In the courtyards of the complex are three domes that recall those of Edwin Lutyens, who designed buildings in New Delhi in a mix of British and Indian styles.

Le Medi Rotterdam

Geurst & Schulze 2009

'Fusion' is the word that Jeroen Geurst used for Le Medi, a complex of 93 housing units he designed in Rotterdam. In Le Medi Jeroen Geurst and his practice Geurst & Schulze sought to achieve a general Dutch-Mediterranean style that appeals to natives and ethnic minorities of all persuasions and ages – everyone, in other words.

Le Medi began as an initiative by the Rotterdam entrepreneur Abderrahman Hassani Idrissi. He wanted houses that would be attractive to ethnic minorities. But it was not to become a Moroccan neighbourhood. His initiative was taken up by the Rotterdam housing association Woonbron Maasoevers, who enlisted the services of property developer ERA Bouw for the project.

The entrance gate of Le Medi leads into a large courtyard surrounded by a covered walkway. From this courtyard you can access two lesser courts and four straight passages leading to smaller gates. Le Medi has its fair share of decorations of both Dutch and foreign origin. In fitting out the large courtyard Geurst & Schulze drew heavily on the piazzas of Venice, the ultimate fusion-city.

Fusion Amsterdam

Marlies Rohmer 2009

'Fusion' is the name Marlies Rohmer gives the multifunctional building she designed in Amsterdam's Oost quarter. The brick exterior with its variety of brickwork bonds refers not only to the decorativeness of Amsterdam School architecture found in abundance round about the centre, but also to the richly ornate architecture of Islam. In 2010 fusion became an official term to denote a style in Dutch architecture when Wilfried van Winden published the manifesto 'Fusion. An appeal for a decorative architecture'. Closely allied as it is to postmodernism as defined by Robert Venturi and Denise Scott Brown back in 1966, fusion is further evidence that post-modernism is flourishing in the multicultural Netherlands.

De Grote Hof Nootdorp

Rapp+Rapp 2007

De Grote Hof in Nootdorp is the biggest of the new *hofjes*, or courtyards of housing, to be built in the Netherlands in the past 20 years. This project of 246 housing units designed by Rapp+Rapp has one large residential courtyard surrounded by four smaller ones. The German architect Christian Rapp, who began his career in this country as co-architect with Hans Kollhoff of the Piraeus building in Amsterdam, has given the principal courtyard an all-round sheltered walkway marked by narrow columns that recall the early, neo-rationalist work of Aldo Rossi. From outside, the complex has a bastion-like appearance, hence its nickname 'The Fort'.
The *hofje*, originally a seventeenth-century building type generally for housing the poor, mostly women, made a remarkable comeback in the Vinex settlements. It is one of the forms of the 'new seclusion' with which property developers and builders sought to meet the increasing desire for a safe home. Other prevalent means of giving residents a feeling of security in the digital age include neighbourhoods on islands and castle-like apartment complexes, preferably surrounded by water.

The New Seclusion

Chapter 7

While the American journalist Christopher Hawthorne, writing in 2004 in *The New York Times*, had described the Vinex housing developments, the latest and indeed last large-scale Dutch residential estates, as cool, they had long had a terrible reputation at home. A few years after the 'Supplement to the Fourth Policy Document on Spatial Planning' was published in 1991, its Dutch acronym Vinex had already come to stand for everything that was dull and monotonous about Dutch suburbia. When the first clumps of housing made their appearance at many places throughout the Netherlands in the second half of the 1990s, Vinex had even become a term of abuse and the critics were merciless. 'In essence they are mean little 1960s dwellings decked out in borrowed finery: a Trabant dolled up to look like an Opel, a Mercedes or a Citroën, according to the buyer's fancy. But underneath it remains a Trabant.' Thus wrote Adri Duivesteijn, then still a Labour (PvdA) member of the Dutch Lower House and former director of the Netherlands Architecture Institute, in the *Architecture in the Netherlands Yearbook 1998/99*. The critics Hilde de Haan and Ids Haagsma went a stage further that same year in de Volkskrant: today's Vinex settlements would be tomorrow's ghettoes.

Duivesteijn and Haagsma and De Haan had set the tone. Their opinion that Vinex would never amount to a thing was taken up not just by the intelligentsia, who had always felt a revulsion for suburbia, but also by politicians. 'Vinex – we won't make that mistake again', said Sybilla Dekker, then Minister of Housing, Spatial Planning and the Environment when taking office in 2003. Her ministry kept its word. After the Vinex settlements, there were no further large-scale housing estates at sites decided on by the authorities. At the start of the twenty-first century, national government abandoned the idea that it should play a key role in spatial planning. Under the banner of 'centralize what we have to and decentralize what we can', spatial planning now became largely a job for municipalities and provinces. This brought an end to 60 years of government-driven housing in the Netherlands.

Amazingly, the Vinex project, the largest building project in the Golden Age of Dutch architecture, made a promising start, even for the critics. When the third cabinet under Ruud Lubbers specified in the Supplement of 1991 that 750,000 housing units were to be built at a 100 or so sites across the Netherlands between 1995 and 2005, most reactions were positive. This was the opportunity to give shape to the 'compact city', was the opinion of urban planners, architects and administrators. Since almost all the Vinex settlements were to be close by the major cities, this would reduce live-work traffic and, therefore, motorway congestion. Not just that, they reasoned, in having a higher density than usual the settlements would acquire a more 'urban' character than the older suburbs. An added advantage of this was that they would make less inroads on the Dutch countryside than their predecessors.

Although most Vinex settlements are still awaiting completion, we can already conclude that neither goal has been reached. With the odd exception, the settlements can not be described as compact. The property developers, who were largely responsible for building them, ultimately decided out of market considerations on an average density of 25 per hectare – the same density as the new build estates of the 1970s and 1980s.

The Vinex settlements were equally unsuccessful in reducing traffic jams. Their authors had not foreseen that Vinex-dwellers would be hypermobile 'urban networkers'. Other than the earlier suburbans, urban networkers are not geared to the city centre in their daily life, but take themselves by car to a range of destinations in the wider surroundings, in

this way assembling their own city, as it were.
At the end of the day the Vinex settlements have fallen between two stools: they are not urban but nor are they truly suburban. The disappointment felt by the Vinex critics can be largely explained by this lack of commitment. Not that this means that they are right. Anyone taking an in-depth look at the settlements has to conclude that they are seldom dull and monotonous suburbs. Indeed, the variety among the Vinex settlements in both urban and architectural terms is far greater than that of any of the older post-war suburbs. The housing density varies from five housing units per hectare in, say, Haverleij outside Den Bosch to 40 in Roomburg, a design made by the City of Leiden. Add to that the fact that in most Vinex developments there are major differences between the neighbourhoods that comprise them. This is certainly true of the larger examples, such as Leidsche Rijn near Utrecht and IJburg in Amsterdam, which have had neighbourhoods designed for them with their own character and ambience, from metropolitan to rustic. So you are unlikely to get lost in a Vinex settlement, which cannot be said of the labyrinthine 'cauliflower resorts' of the 1980s.

There is a similarly wide variety in architectural styles, from neo-traditionalist to neo-modernist and from the mundane to the exotic. And although terraced housing prevails in most Vinex settlements, the dwelling types are much more diverse than in the older suburbs. In Vinexland you can see contemporary canal houses a stone's throw away from contemporary dyke houses and urban villas alongside time-honoured row houses.

But the Vinex developments have common traits as well. Many of their designers have set out to give them their own identity by stepping off from the existing landscape. Paradoxically, this has ultimately led to a degree of uniformity: the simple fact that much of the Netherlands consists of polders with their grids of main and transverse channels means that almost all Vinex settlements have their quota of waterside dwellings.

Even more remarkable is a phenomenon that during the past 15 years has been making inroads into the old and new parts of Dutch cities, namely the 'new seclusion'. Just about every Vinex settlement contains more or less closed-off complexes that recall the courtyard housing in the old town centres. Ypenburg near The Hague, for example, has a number of such residential courts, including De Grote Hof (architect Rapp+Rapp), a vast bastion-like ensemble with five enclosed communal gardens.

The new seclusion has yet to lead in the Netherlands to genuine gated communities, walled secure residential enclaves such as the US and other Western countries have had for 30 years. It did produce a large number of buildings and estates resembling castles or bastions. The success of Brandevoort, the Helmond Vinex settlement with a fortified town at its centre, has been repeated many times, often by Rob Krier himself. And Haverleij when complete will combine a fortified town and nine residential 'castles', all surrounded by a moat.

It is no coincidence that the new seclusion emerged at the same time as neo-traditionalism. The two phenomena have the same roots and are often found together. For many in this country globalization, besides fostering a desire for the individual and unique, has also created a sense of insecurity in light of the rapid social changes. Although police statistics tell us that robberies and physical violence have steadily decreased during the age of globalization, today's citizen is often fearful: the lack of safety, not least at the social level, is one of the digital citizen's greatest worries, so it transpired time and again from population surveys made around the turn of the millennium. The new castles and courtyard housing are to allay this fear and give urban networkers the feeling that they have a secure home base from which to engage on the wide-ranging activities of their daily lives.

The Whale Amsterdam

Frits van Dongen/de Architekten Cie. 2000

Striking buildings sometimes earn themselves a nickname before being completed. Some of these names are more flattering than others, which is why clients and architects increasingly took to thinking up names themselves for their 'icons' during the building boom of the past quarter century. Often these are English. For example, Frits van Dongen's superblock, sited amongst the high-density low rise on Borneo-Sporenburg, was called The Whale, although it is not exactly clear why. There is nothing organic about its form, in fact the grey zinc-clad building is all angles.

This whale stands face-to-face with the Piraeus building on KNSM-eiland, the most influential building in the golden quarter century of Dutch architectural history. The similarity between the two is uncanny: Piraeus (1994), designed by the Germans Hans Kollhoff and Christian Rapp, was the first block to be built in the Netherlands with an inward-sloping roof, giving it a striking sculptural form. The Whale seeks to go one better. Not only does its roof fall and rise more precipitously than that of its neighbour across the water, the entire building is lifted into space. Originally the design included a publicly accessible courtyard garden, but the housing corporation managing the building, Lieven de Key, decided against this idea for administrative reasons.

KC Noord Utrecht
VMX Architects 2006

The Vinex era brought with it a new building type, whose name (brede school) translates as 'extended school' or 'community school'. More than just a school, it is a multi-purpose building with amenities serving the local community (school, crèche, library, sports hall, etcetera). Of more importance than its multifunctional role, however, is the proviso that its rooms are able to facilitate a change of function. Having learnt from the fact that many schools in neighbourhoods with an ageing population have fallen into disuse, housing associations and other clients now sought more flexible 'community schools' that could even accept housing in the future. These community or extended schools occur in Vinex settlements in all forms and styles. In KC Noord, the community school serving Vleuterweide, part of the Leidsche Rijn settlement, VMX Architects assembled a sports hall, a crèche, a school and other amenities in an impressive neo-modernist building. As the radiant hub of the neighbourhood, KC Noord is a community centre worthy of the name.

Patio Island The Hague
John Bosch 2002

Just as MVRDV had given a new twist to the patio dwelling type in their part of Patio Island, an island in The Hague Vinex settlement of Ypenburg, so John Bosch invented a new type of courtyard housing in the area allotted to him. Bosch's ensemble of 144 housing units breaks down into five larger and four smaller residential courts. The courts are less introverted than usual, being something like a cross between the regular streets in a neighbourhood of terraced housing and an old-fashioned residential courtyard.
Broad footpaths and cycle-ways traverse the central yards and pass through the broad entryways to the courts, giving the ensemble a semi-public and somewhat open character. Interestingly Bosch dispensed with a gradual transition between the private domain of the dwellings and the shared central yards, whose lawns extend right up to the front doors. This sharp division between private and communal is driven home by the taut vivid green cladding on the courtyard walls.

Patio Island The Hague

MVRDV 2004

Few Dutch practices are as adept in combining familiar dwelling types in unexpected ways as MVRDV. On Patio Island in Ypenburg they have crossed the time-honoured Dutch row house with the patio dwelling to give patio row houses. But MVRDV's greatest strength is that it succeeds in pushing certain phenomena and typologies in architecture and urban planning to their outermost limits.
Their patio dwellings on an island in Ypenburg are an extreme expression of the new seclusion. As housing goes, MVRDV's contribution is as defensive as it gets. The walls are clad from top to bottom in black slate and even the entrances to the houses are camouflaged with the same material. The dwellings in this walled neighbourhood are as self-communing as can be. 'Patio Island is as private as a gated community', as the authors of *MVRDV Buildings* (2013) put it. So is this in fact the Netherlands' first gated community?

Hagen Island The Hague

MVRDV 2001

At times when considering a project by MVRDV one cannot help wondering whether it is meant seriously or as a joke. One such case is Hagen Island, the neighbourhood they designed in Ypenburg. The joke of the row houses and semi's on this island is that their exteriors (walls and roofs alike) are without exception made of one and the same material.
Thus, for example, one house is entirely of vivid blue cladding panels, another of red roofing tiles and yet another has exterior walls of silver-grey aluminium. This makes them look like houses a toddler might draw, giving the unsettling feeling that they are a parody of the age-old Dutch row houses. Or did MVRDV do this to make them look good in photographs and guarantee them attention in the media?
The floor plans of the row houses on Hagen Island are standard: the architecture goes no further than the exterior. In planning terms, however, the island deviates from the average neighbourhood of terraced housing. There are no streets. It is as if the row houses have been cut out and scattered across the site. Cars have been banned to the perimeter, so that many homes can only be reached on foot.

Crystal Court Amsterdam
TANGRAM Architecten 2009

Trays became the 'in' thing during the last decades of the twentieth century: more and more buildings were given bigger and bigger appurtenances. The absolute peak of the trend for trays was MVRDV's Oklahoma sheltered housing (1997), a box of apartments with five gigantic trays jutting from it in a quite terrifying attempt to defy the laws of nature.
Fashions usually vanish once they have reached their peak. But the tray trend persisted even after Oklahoma was completed in Amsterdam's Nieuw-West quarter and reached a new peak in 2009 with Crystal Court, an apartment building designed by the Dutch firm of TANGRAM in Buitenveldert, in the south of the city. The building's name comes from the glass atrium nestling between the stacked jutting boxes.
It is with this complex stacking of boxes that Crystal Court forges a link between the older tray trend and a new one: pixel architecture. This international architectural vogue can take on different forms. Sometimes pixel architecture gets no further than wacky facades of metal or polystyrene squares in different colours and patterns. But some pixel buildings, such as MVRDV's DNB Bank headquarters (2012) in Oslo, are accumulations of small cubes that recall the structuralist buildings of the 1960s and 1970s by the likes of Herman Hertzberger.

L O U W M A N
DISCOVER GHIBLI

Cockpit Utrecht

ONL 2008

The Cockpit car showroom is part of a long acoustic barrier, also designed by ONL (Kas Oosterhuis), along the A2 motorway. Constructed of steel bars and transparent panels, the barrier twists and turns much as one would expect from a computer architect. The Cockpit, assembled from curved glass triangles, marks a swelling in the barrier, giving it the appearance of a snake that has just polished off its prey.
The Wall, a ‘Ferrari red’ complex designed by Fons Verheijen, attaches to ONL’s acoustic barrier in the south. It too is an undulating structure with a double duty as acoustic barrier and shopping centre. The fate of The Wall illustrates the crisis that crippled the Dutch real estate market after the credit crunch of 2008. After opening in that year much of The Wall remained empty. Three years later the proprietor went bankrupt and the building was taken over by the real estate branch of the SNS Bank. At the start of 2013 the SNS Bank itself got into difficulties after recklessly investing in what turned out to be worthless real estate and was nationalized. The Wall has been state property ever since.

Witte Kaap Amsterdam

Claus en Kaan Architecten 2010

With their razor-sharp, neo-modernist buildings Felix Claus and Kees Kaan found themselves dubbed the 'kings of Dutch minimalism'. But this does their work little justice. Line up all their buildings and it is clear that Claus and Kaan (who are now no longer partners) were eclectics. Their 'house of culture and administration' (2007) in Nijverdal is neo-traditionalist whereas their care cluster in the Roombeek area of Enschede with its cascade of balconies belongs in the tradition of Amsterdam School expressionism.

Witte Kaap, a large housing block in the Amsterdam Vinex settlement of IJburg, straddles the boundary between minimalism and Amsterdam School. Its stepped form and particularly the treatment of the sharp corner resembling a luxury liner are references to The Ship (1920), the celebrated Amsterdam School building in that city's Spaarndammer neighbourhood. But unlike The Ship's architect, Michel de Klerk, Claus and Kaan have dispensed with decoration and given their building the taut appearance of an ocean-going liner.

Water Dwellings

Amsterdam

Marlies Rohmer 2011

Water is a key component of many Vinex settlements. Builders discovered that living along or on the water was a highly prized commodity. This explains the profusion of water channels in a variety of sizes in these settlements.
IJburg, the Amsterdam Vinex development built in the waters of IJmeer, even has its own lake, scooped from the sand fill of Steigereiland, the IJburg island closest to Amsterdam. Moored in this lake is the country's largest water-borne residential area to a design by Marlies Rohmer. The 75 water dwellings form a close-knit neighbourhood, nestling behind Liesbeth van der Pol's live-work building.
All houses in this floating neighbourhood have a cladding of prefabricated plastic panels. There are three types of water dwelling, although they all look the same, the way shipping containers do. Front and rear are invariably glazed. The opaque side walls are in subdued colours such as mustard and blue-grey. Interiors are freely subdivisible.

Parkrand Amsterdam

MVRDV 2007

With renewal of the residential areas of the nineteenth century and the first half of the twentieth nearing completion around 1990, it was the turn of those areas built during the post-war reconstruction. One drawback of many post-war housing estates, at least according to the administrators of housing associations and cities at that time, was that they had too much public space. Most often built to the modernist precepts of light, air and space, they had too many areas that, in effect, belonged to nobody.
The new housing blocks erected as part of the 'urban restructuring' programme for the post-war areas were to fill up this reserve space. Many of them were given enclosed gardens or courtyards that were for residents only. Thus the new seclusion made its entry into the modernist housing estates with their open plan layouts. MVRDV would not have been MVRDV if they hadn't given the perimeter block a new twist. Their Parkrand project in Amsterdam's Nieuw-West quarter consequently isn't a perimeter block at all but a box with huge holes punched in it, exposing the enclosed garden on the first floor to all and sundry.

The Makeable Society

Chapter 8

Second only to the Vinex settlements in the building projects stakes during the Golden Age of Dutch architecture was what was called 'urban restructuring' (stedelijke vernieuwing). In the decades flanking century's end, developments built onto the major cities after the Second World War were rigorously 'restructured'. In many cases this meant wholesale demolition followed by new build.

The statistics are impressive. To restructure Amsterdam's 'Western Garden Suburbs' (Westelijke Tuinsteden), the most famous of all Dutch post-war residential areas and designed to the functionalist principles of light, air and space, meant demolishing 13,000 housing units alone. Eventually, 24,000 new homes will have been built in their stead, 70 per cent freehold and up-market rented units and 30 per cent social rented units.

Urban restructuring is the successor to the urban renewal of the 1970s and 1980s. This large-scale operation had mainly been devoted to improving residential areas built around the centre of the major cities during the years 1870–1940. At the end of the 1980s, as the urban renewal programme neared its end after 25 years of demolishing, building and renovating, the owners of dwellings in the post-war estates concluded that these were now due for extensive refurbishment. Without it, many areas dating from the reconstruction era would deteriorate into 'ghettoes for the disadvantaged'. At least this was the concern of those running the housing associations, as these owned the lion's share of housing in the post-war areas.

Built in the years 1945–1970, the 'light, air and space' estates were much loved at the time. For their first residents, often coming from small, over-full houses in the city centres and old neighbourhoods, this was literally a new and better world. In 1990, however, the government's overspill development policy had seen most of the original occupants move out to row houses in overspill municipalities like Almere, Purmerend and Zoetermeer. Minority ethnic communities took their place so that many post-war development areas became one-sidedly multicultural (the Dutch term is *zwart*, 'black'). Meanwhile many of the social rented units in these areas no longer met the changed demands. This prompted the housing associations to conclude that demolish and rebuild was often the only option.

Space was another problem afflicting the reconstruction-era estates. The administrators felt that the excessive public space often typifying such areas no longer worked. If these originally represented the shining future that the post-war reconstruction would bring, by millennium's end the indeterminate open areas 'belonging to nobody' evoked feelings of unsafety among many residents.

When urban restructuring began in the 1990s, the generally implicit goal was to create a social mix in the post-war areas. The strategy of replacing much of the dilapidated, cramped social rented housing with owner-occupied properties and more up-market rented units was to lure back the white middle-class. At the end of the 1990s, however, on completion of the first new units the areas proved impossible to 'whiten': the ethnic minorities stayed put and presented an ever expanding majority. The urban restructurers, being of a practical mind, then set a new objective: the middle class should be able to remain living in the reconstruction-era estates, period. Residents, 'black' or 'white', who became more affluent and could afford more than a social rented unit should then be able to move into a larger, more expensive home in their own area.

Even the reformulated objective of urban restructuring attested to an anachronistic faith in a socially engineered society. The widely held conviction among politicians and administrators that the age of government intervention was over was not shared by the urban restructurers. They still saw architecture, or 'stacking bricks' as they themselves often called it, as a way to change the world. Even a decentralizing national government, which in the years around the turn of the millennium had transferred all manner of traditional government duties including energy supply to the private sector, demonstrated a continuing belief in a 'makeable' society. In 1998 the Second Cabinet under Wim Kok appointed a minister without portfolio whose responsibilities included the 'major cities integration policy'. Nine years later, the then Minister of Integration and Housing Ella Vogelaar earmarked 40 'problem' areas for additional investments in urban restructuring. These were soon dubbed 'Vogelaar neighbourhoods – the minister herself used the terms 'jewel' or 'action' neighbourhoods.

Urban restructuring was well under way in some residential areas when Minister Vogelaar took office. All the same, many Vogelaar neighbourhoods could better be described as Vinexed rather than restructured. Amsterdam's Western Garden Suburbs, for example, often proudly touted as 'the largest restructuring area in Europe', were graced with new build in a whole range of styles by the cream of Dutch architects including Liesbeth van der Pol, Meyer en Van Schooten, Wiel Arets, Marlies Rohmer and Claus en Kaan. There we see Wiel Arets' quartet of cool intractable towers (2009) in Osdorp locking into the original modernist architecture of the Western Garden Suburbs, while Liesbeth van der Pol's red-brick residential sculpture (2010) in the Van Tijen neighbourhood refers instead to the architecture of the Amsterdam School. Ironically, this last-named style was denounced by the moralistic modernist Cornelis van Eesteren, who had been chiefly responsible for masterplanning the Western Garden Suburbs, as 'deceitful'.

The new seclusion has also made its mark on the Western Garden Suburbs and other urban restructuring areas. Noorderhof (1999) for example, a small neighbourhood designed by Rob Krier near the central lake (Sloterplas), with its traditional streets of passive facades and the small square alongside Granpré Molière's Pius X church is the complete antithesis of Van Eesteren's modern urban planning. Less extreme but just as secluded is Hof van Hoytema (2003) designed by Heren 5 architecten. In this courtyard housing the central space is fenced off to all but the residents. Another design from that same year to have closed-off courts is FARO's Geuzentuinen. Even the supermodernist Parkrand (2007) designed by MVRDV, a firm with an even greater aversion to traditionalism than Van Eesteren, has an elevated 'garden' for residents only.

The most pressing question after 20 years of urban restructuring is of course whether the often rigorous demolish and rebuild strategy has worked. Is it still possible to 'make' society? Not in the opinion of sociologists like Jan Willem Duyvendak. They feel that you won't solve the problems of those living in 'jewel' neighbourhoods by demolishing their homes and bringing in the middle class. It doesn't provide jobs for the unemployed or get junkies to kick the habit. To refute this criticism the administrators of housing associations and local councils can always point to the figures in such fact-finding studies as 'Quality of Life in the Balance' (Leefbaarheid in Balans) carried out in 2011 by RIGO Research. Generally, the residents of 'Vogelaar neighbourhoods' have given these a higher score since they were restructured; they now feel safer and more at home.

These high ratings notwithstanding, urban restructuring has now reached an impasse. The 2008 credit crunch had slowed down many such projects or seen them shelved. To compound matters, there were to be no more investments by national government after 2014. And so urban restructuring, a most anachronistic revival of the belief in a makeable society, is quietly leaving the stage.

Oklahoma Sheltered Housing Amsterdam

MVRDV 1997

Appurtenances on buildings were very much in vogue in Dutch architecture of the mid 1990s. But the enormous trays protruding from this block of sheltered housing (Dutch acronym WoZoCo) in Osdorp in the south-east of the city were only partly dictated by fashion. According to the architects, it was also a question of arithmetic. The volume allowed at that site as stipulated in the 1950s by the designers of the Western Garden Suburbs could only accept 84 apartments for the over-55s instead of the 100 required by the client. So the architects of MVRDV slung five colossal trays from the permitted volume to accommodate the 16 missing apartments.
The rear of the WoZoCo complex is dotted with rectangular balconies, many of whose balustrades are of brightly coloured glass (purple, orange or blue).

OKLAHOMA

Pontanusstraat Housing Amsterdam
Liesbeth van der Pol 1992

The urban renewal in Amsterdam's Pontanusstraat was one of Liesbeth van der Pol's first built projects. Like so many other architects of her generation who graduated in the 1980s, her first commission came from a housing association. Housing associations were more aware than other clients of the fact that domestic construction is as much a cultural task. From their earliest years they invited the best architects to design workers' housing. Thus began the Dutch tradition that saw the greatest names in architecture engaged on mass housing. From Berlage to Rem Koolhaas – virtually all the Dutch architectural giants have designed social housing.
This tradition is now in danger of disappearing thanks to the ongoing liberalization of the housing market. With the role of the housing associations as commissioning bodies slipping away, the end of social housing has been announced in so many words.

Row Houses on Domela Nieuwenhuisstraat Amsterdam
Atelier Kempe Thill 2008

For a long time it seemed as though the *doorzonwoning*, or through-by-light house, could not be improved upon. All the same, German architects André Kempe and Oliver Thill created a new take on the row house during the restructuring of the modernist Western Garden Suburbs. Their dwellings have the minimum width prescribed by the Building Decree: 4.8 metres. In order to achieve an acceptable area of living space, they are deeper than the traditional through-by-light house. In the interests of sufficient daylight the front facades are almost entirely of glass.
The greatest difference with the *doorzonwoning* is that the internal subdivision has been radically revised. Living has been relocated to the first floor, with a garage and the kitchen up front on the ground floor. This puts paid to the through-room aspect, the glazed facades notwithstanding.

Dedemsvaartweg Apartment Block

The Hague

Art Zaaijer and Kees Christiaanse/OMA 1992

The City of The Hague felt that urban restructuring should be a festive affair. So at the end of the 1980s, when the number of new homes built in that city was nearing the 200,000 mark, the Municipal Executive decided to celebrate this fact with a 'housing festival' in Morgenstond, a post-war reconstruction area in the south-west of the city. Kees Christiaanse and Art Zaaijer, who were still with OMA at the time, drew up the urban master plan for the festival site, an unbuilt strip along Dedemsvaartweg. Famous architects from home and abroad including Josep Lluís Mateo, Arquitectonica and Rem Koolhaas filled out the strip, with Christiaanse and Zaaijer themselves contributing an apartment building with big holes punched in it, one of the earliest examples of the vogue for holes. The entire festival project took over two decades to complete, which dampened the party spirits somewhat.

Montevideo Rotterdam

Mecanoo 2005

At Kop van Zuid, Rotterdam's most prestigious urban restructuring project and 25 years in the making, a coterie of foreign architects contributed a building apiece. Sir Norman Foster, far and away England's most famous architect, designed the World Port Center, the Italian Renzo Piano the KPN Telecom office building, the German firm of Bolles+Wilson the red Luxor Theater and the Portuguese Álvaro Siza a skyscraper, New Orleans.

It's a remarkable fact that no foreign architect has ever produced their best work in the Netherlands. At Kop van Zuid the foreigners have once again failed to impress. The most successful of the bunch is New Orleans, Siza's take on the classic American skyscraper from the first half of the twentieth century. Like Cass Gilbert's Woolworth Building in New York (1913), New Orleans boasts a thoughtfully crafted crown.

Francine Houben of Mecanoo claims that the classic sky-scrapers of Chicago and New York likewise inspired Montevideo. But her tower is altogether different from Siza's, being more a collage of wide-ranging elements than a single vertical entity.

Het Bastion Amsterdam

Dam & Partners 2006

Cees Dam is the lone wolf of Dutch architecture. He has never belonged to a group of like-minded architects, nor has he ever worked in one specific style. Throughout his career he has been an eclectic who has ridden roughshod over vogues and trends in architecture. He was not afraid of designing in a grand style at a time when many of his colleagues associated monumentality with the Albert Speer approach, and was not averse to postmodernism when this was lumped together with rats and deadly epidemics. Het Bastion, which Dam designed with his son Diederik, is an out-of-left-field contribution to the urban restructuring of Osdorp, one of Amsterdam's Western Garden Suburbs. The name suggests that Dam's building is a housing block with an enclosed courtyard. But this is exactly what it is not. The triangular central court atop a parking facility is shaped by three volumes, one of which sports a tall, broad entryway. This does have a full-width fence but its gate is always open during the day.

Book Mountain

Spijkenisse
MVRDV 2012

For many years MVRDV was known as a purveyor of 'fuck the context' architecture. But recently the firm has also been making contextual work, such as Book Mountain, the new public library of Spijkenisse, south-west of Rotterdam.
On the one hand Book Mountain – a pyramid of walls clad with bookshelves – is vintage MVRDV. Originally, the architects wanted to place the library under a glass dome. In the end, though, the glazed enclosure was given the form of a building with a hipped roof, a reference to the old barns with such roofs still found in the town centre. So Book Mountain is as much contextual as it is expressive of its purpose.
Next door to Book Mountain is a residential neighbourhood, also designed by MVRDV, whose housing units cluster about a car-free square at the old village church of Spijkenisse. All dwellings have gabled roofs, with both roofs and external walls in the same red brick as the base of the library. Book Mountain and the small neighbourhood are in turn part of the project to renovate the centre of Spijkenisse to a design by Soeters Van Eldonk architecten. Normally, MVRDV and Sjoerd Soeters are worlds apart in the architecture they design. But in Spijkenisse MVRDV's brick 'architecture parlante' has no quarrel with the new 'Old Dutch' city centre.

Harp, Lute and Zither Haarlemmermeer

Santiago Calatrava 2004

Beautiful is difficult, so why take the easy way? This is the motto of the Spanish architect Santiago Calatrava and it has worked very well for him. His ingenious museums, skyscrapers and most especially bridges inspired by skeletons have been built on almost every continent. And they are almost invariably iconic. The Municipality of Haarlemmermeer west of Amsterdam commissioned Calatrava to design three iconic bridges over the principal canal or Hoofdvaart. Calatrava made all three complex sculptures of tall pylons and many cables.
Harp, Lute and Zither are wonderful to behold, but also grotesque. The crossings of this none too wide canal have been designed to within an inch of their lives. They were controversial even before construction began: a number of councillors were opposed to the additional costs incurred by the icons. Not long after completion all three began to show signs of rust.

Zuidtangent Bus Terminal Hoofddorp

NIO architecten 2003

As the twenty-first century dawned buildings increasingly took on sculptural forms. Those sculptures recalled the expressionist buildings of the Amsterdam School of around 1920. So neo-expressionism is a good name for the new sculptural architecture.
Although the bus station in Hoofddorp for the Zuidtangent line is little more than a few small rooms and a roofed area for waiting, it has become a 50-metre-long blob which, like so many blobs, brings to mind some form of animal life, in this case a mollusc. Completed in 2003, this building designed by Maurice Nio was proclaimed the 'world's largest synthetic material sculpture'. It was also one of the first blobs to be constructed not from rectangular panels but from blocks of polystyrene foam carved by a computer-controlled milling machine.

Vesteda Tower

Eindhoven

Jo Coenen 2006

Architectural history has always been a network of allied buildings and the decades flanking the turn of the millennium were little different. Despite the rise of the starchitect phenomenon and the accompanying greater importance accorded to originality in the age of postmodernism, most architects are still standing on the shoulders of their predecessors and contemporaries. For example, Jo Coenen's residential tower block in Eindhoven is a variation on the world-famous Flatiron Building in New York.

The form architect Daniel Burnham gave his New York smoothing iron of 1903 was dictated by its location at Madison Square, where Broadway, the only long street not to adhere to the Manhattan grid, meets Fifth Avenue at an acute angle. Coenen's own flatiron also occupies a narrow plot, although the one on Smalle Haven in Eindhoven is less coercive than the one in New York: it could have accommodated a differently shaped narrow volume. Coenen instead opted to duplicate the Flatiron Building. He even followed the Classical tripartition of Burnham's masterpiece, with a tall base of offices, a long shaft of identical upper storeys and a clearly articulated capital, which in Eindhoven contains double-height penthouses.

Not just an architect who reuses famous examples, Coenen is himself an heir to the modernist skyscraper architects: his Eindhoven tower is almost entirely devoid of decoration. If Burnham designed his Flatiron as an ornate stretched take on a Renaissance palazzo, the frontage of Coenen's smoothing iron is, with the exception of a vertical thrust in cut stone, a simple glazed concrete grid.

Laan van Spartaan Amsterdam

Claus en Kaan Architecten, Dick van Gameren et al. 2014

Laan van Spartaan marks the end of an era in two respects. The immense ensemble, designed by a regiment of architects, is the largest new complex to be built as part of the urban restructuring programme for Amsterdam's Nieuw-West quarter. Sited around the sports fields of De Spartaan soccer club, its thousands of housing units in many types and price brackets are joined by a school, a health care organization, a supermarket, a dental practice, a badminton club, a circus, a sports hall and an indoor climbing gym. Laan van Spartaan is also the last urban restructuring complex of this size. Since the building crisis broke in 2008 and national government withdrew all further subsidies, urban restructuring has been relegated to the back burner. Laan van Spartaan also marks the end of the long-term vogue for dark brick. This had lasted a full twenty years since 1994, when Kollhoff and Rapp's dark-brown Piraeus block was completed in Amsterdam. In the crisis years post 2008 Dutch architects, including the Laan van Spartaan brigade, shifted their allegiance en masse to light-coloured brick. Curiously, this was also in fashion at the start of the 1980s when the industry was hit by a similarly heavy crisis.

Anton Building Eindhoven

Diederendirrix 2013

For decades the factories of the Philips electronics concern had been Eindhoven's very own Forbidden City. Occupying a large zone (Strijp-S) near the city centre, the giant company buildings were fenced off as an enclave accessible to Philips workers only.
But now that Philips has stopped production in many of its factories, and has long had its headquarters in Amsterdam, Eindhoven is steadily transforming into a city with a mix of dwellings, work and recreation. So Philips' departure has proved to be a blessing in disguise for Eindhoven. It did mean mass unemployment but Eindhoven as a city is the better for it. The Witte Dame or White Lady (1931), for example, designed in the middle of the town centre by Dirk Roosenburg as a monofunctional light bulb factory, now houses a cultural centre, including the Design Academy, since its conversion by Diederendirrix, which was completed in 1998.
The Anton Building, an imposing edifice originally designed as an appliances factory (1930) by Philips' own building department, is an addition to the new, undivided Eindhoven. Anton like the Witte Dame is a national monument that has been refurbished by the Eindhoven architects Diederendirrix. And like the old light bulb factory, Paul Diederen and Bert Dirrix have limited themselves in Anton to a few well-aimed interventions that have left the exterior of the white factory building almost entirely intact.

Villa Van Kooten

Almere

Commandeur Haumann architecten 2012

The new polder settlement of Almere became the row house capital of the Netherlands. Its construction began in the 1970s, just as the flats of Bijlmermeer, the apotheosis of modernist urbanism south-east of Amsterdam, emerged as the biggest urban planning disaster in Dutch history. The failure of Bijlmermeer meant no more suburbs presided over by high rises. That course was abandoned and row houses took over, as they did in Almere.
But then the row house itself came under fire. In 1997 the then chairman of the Union of Dutch Architects spearheaded the attack on the row house in an interview in *NRC Handelsblad*. In the neoliberal era the collectivist row house was old hat. It was high time that Dutch domestic construction adapted to the neoliberal Zeitgeist and that the deregulated housing market known as Wilde Wonen became the norm. Anyone wanting to buy a plot and have their house built on it should be in a position to do so. Labour politician and Lower House member Adri Duivesteijn took over the Wilde Wonen concept from its deviser Carel Weeber. When he became Almere's alderman for Spatial Planning and Housing in 2006, he persuaded the council to allow Wilde Wonen free rein in new residential areas such as Homeruskwartier. Thus Almere changed from the country's pre-eminent row house city into the capital of Wilde Wonen.

The Failed Revolution

Chapter 9

We know the exact day when Wilde Wonen was conceived. On 7 April 1997 the term featured as the heading of an interview in *NRC Handelsblad* with Carel Weeber, architect and co-founder of de Architekten Cie. and at that time chairman of the Union of Dutch Architects.

Wilde Wonen was literally an overnight success. The next day, *De Telegraaf*, the country's biggest selling daily newspaper, reported that none other than the chairman of the architects' union had called for a revolution in housing: everyone in the Netherlands should be able to have their own house built, with or without the help of an architect.

In the interview Weeber called for the end of what he called 'state architecture'. Throughout almost the entire twentieth century, he explained, the state had played a major part in domestic construction by giving subsidies to housing associations. The upshot was that after the Second World War the row house was the most prevalent dwelling type in the Netherlands. This was when the majority of the population expressed a preference for a detached home. And now, he observed, the Vinex settlements in the making were filling up with mainly row houses. This was absurd in the age of globalization, liberalization and a government in retreat: why didn't the authorities simply give those who wanted to have their own house built the opportunity to do so?

Weeber's call for Wilde Wonen came with a cut-and-dried plan he had drawn up with a property developer. 'It's very simple,' he explained. 'The government issues 25 plots per hectare. Roads run along one side of those plots. The government prescribes that 60 per cent of each of the plots abutting the road may be developed and 80 per cent of the strips abutting the other plots must consist of gardens. Other than that, the landowners are free to build as they please. My ideal is that they visit a do-it-yourself retailer, much like our Gamma hardware chain, that sells government-approved home components in a number of varieties.'

Besides being a revolution in urban planning and housing, Wilde Wonen was also to be an aesthetic revolution. A century of state architecture had brought about a state aesthetic, according to Weeber: 'The Modern Movement of Mies van der Rohe and all those others has always had ties with the authorities: first this style was propagated by German social-democratic governments and after the Second World War it was adopted by governments all over Europe. But what the state likes isn't always what the public likes. There's a big gap between the two. If you look inside all those houses designed by state architects they're full of traditional oak furniture. It's only the homes of architects and others in the know whose exteriors don't clash with the interiors: these have the dutiful Corbusier and Rietveld furniture.'

It seems that Wilde Wonen could not have arrived at a better moment. In the Netherlands as elsewhere in the 1990s, many politicians, even those of a social-democratic persuasion, had become convinced that the market worked better than the government. When Ruud Lubbers was Prime Minister the national government was in the throes of liberalizing everything in sight. Housing was no exception: in 1995 the housing associations and corporations were privatized. From then on, they had to carry out their principal task, building and managing social rented units, without government subsidies.

Despite the liberal spirit of the times, Wilde Wonen had a less than warm welcome in architectural circles. Many critics felt that it failed to fit into the Dutch tradition of centralization in planning and housing and aesthetic control in architecture. It would lead to chaos, they predicted, to a gross and ramshackle built environment. They were also afraid of the proliferation of the 'white mould' of generally white free-standing houses found mainly in the open country of Friesland, Zeeland and elsewhere.

All the same, Wilde Wonen seemed destined for success. Some architects, such as Robert Winkel and the duo Daan Bakker and Christian Rapp, designed catalogue houses. Property developers advanced free-ranging, flexible houses that could easily be adapted to the needs of home buyers. In 2001 the municipality of Almere built Gewild Wonen, a model neighbourhood of 550 houses designed by 15 different architects that admittedly were not 'deregulated' but certainly more flexible than usual. (The name is a play on Wilde Wonen but means 'sought-after' instead of deregulated.)

One year earlier it seemed as if Wilde Wonen was even poised to take over as the new state architecture, when the then State Secretary of Housing, the Liberal politician Johan Remkes, in his white paper whose title translates as 'People, wishes, homes' decreed that 30 per cent of the land of yet-to-be-built Vinex settlements had to be issued as 'self-build plots' where buyers could literally build as they pleased.

Almost every Vinex settlement was given a portion where owner-builders could get their own homes built, whether or not with a vetting committee looking over their shoulder. Now that most such areas have been built up, we can conclude that the critics' fears of chaos were unfounded. Most build-it-yourselvers proved to have a predilection for catalogue houses in more or less traditional styles. The self-build neighbourhoods in the Vinex developments are bristling with faux farmhouses, 1930s-style villas and other neo-traditionalist house types. Neo-modernist, neo-expressionist houses and blobs make up a tiny minority.

That the Wilde Wonen revolution ultimately failed was for more than just aesthetic reasons. Despite the government's input to stimulate self-build the number of Wilde Wonen houses built in the Netherlands after Weeber's call for a change of tack, dropped instead of rose. If 11,000 such houses, 16 per cent of the entire housing production, were built in 2000, the year of the white paper on 'People, wishes, homes', three years later this had fallen to 6500 or 11 per cent. In the years that followed, the number of houses built annually by private clients stalled around the 7,000 mark.

Why the Wilde Wonen project failed is easily explained: central government no longer has the power over the housing sector that it once had, having relinquished it by privatizing the housing associations in 1995. Since then central government has been without its means of guiding the housing sector, namely through subsidies and loans.

Add to that the fact that central government and most municipalities do not own the building land. Most of this belongs to property developers and large construction firms. And these make a bigger profit by building houses on that land than by selling it as self-build plots. Another factor is that it is easier for municipalities to reach their housing quota by teaming up with experienced property developers they have long worked with on a regular basis than with unfamiliar private individuals who are having their first house built.

Wilde Wonen was a success in only a few places, invariably the result of extenuating circumstances or strong-willed administrators. In Enschede this private patronage, the official name for Wilde Wonen, was given free rein in Roombeek, an area largely destroyed in 2000 when a fireworks factory exploded. The city's specially set-up Reconstruction Project Office decided that 400 of the 1,500 new homes were to be built by private individuals.

In Almere, one of the few Dutch cities to own its building land, it was the impassioned planning politician Adri Duivesteijn, former director of the Netherlands Architecture Institute and these days Labour member of the Dutch Upper House, who precipitated a revolution in housing. After being appointed Almere's alderman for Spatial Planning and Housing in 2006, he made dramatic changes to local plans for housing. Convinced that citizens have a fundamental right to be able to have their own house built, Duivesteijn introduced 'organic planning', in which private parties and small investors finance and construct the buildings. In his view organic planning not only gives the self-builders the houses they want but also ensures more liveable urban areas than those in Vinex settlements. Thus Almere became the capital city of Wilde Wonen, where private parties are to see onto site 20,000 of the 60,000 housing units that the city plans to build before 2030.

Gewild Wonen Almere

Carel Weeber 2001

Carel Weeber has always insisted that the notion of Wilde Wonen is the result of a misunderstanding. He had mentioned in an interview with *NRC Handelsblad* that the favoured form of dwelling (*gewild wonen*) among most Dutch was the detached house. But the journalist interviewing him had misheard and written down *wilde* (literally, 'wild') instead.
In fact if you read that interview with Weeber from 1997, he makes no mention, misheard or otherwise, of the expression anywhere. It was editor Bianca Stigter who devised the heading 'Het Wilde Wonen'. And the rest is history.
Four years after that interview, a building expo bearing the name 'Gewild Wonen' was opened in the suburb of Almere-Buiten. After holding a competition to design sought-after dwellings the City of Almere invited 20 construction firms to erect a total of 550 'sought-after dwellings' in a model neighbourhood. The dwellings had to be flexible and highly adaptable to meet the wishes of their occupants. One of the architects was Carel Weeber.

Scheepstimmer-manstraat Amsterdam

Various architects 1999

Borneo-Sporenburg, the high-density area of row houses designed by West 8 in Amsterdam's eastern docks area, was another project that included plots for own-home builders. But here again, the 'wild' Wilde Wonen had been tamed: home designs had to comply with all kinds of requirements. Houses had to be no more than 9.2 metres high, with 3.5 metres stipulated for the ground floor height. Plot buyers were additionally obliged to develop the entire plot. And they had to enlist the services of an architect; catalogue houses were taboo. Despite all these demands the houses display an amazing diversity: each architect has solved the puzzle in their own way. Number 120, a house designed by Koen van Velsen, even has a tree in it.
All units on Scheepstimmerman-straat face the water, with almost all street sides giving an impression of enclosure.

Sodae House Amstelveen

Don Murphy/VMX Architects
2009

One of the institutions in Dutch architecture that Carel Weeber was challenging with his Wilde Wonen was Welstand, the local government commission overseeing the 'visual decency' of buildings. This 'architecture police' had no place in the neoliberal age. Weeber's fight against Welstand has only been moderately successful, and only a few Dutch municipalities have abolished it. Don Murphy of VMX Architects found himself up against Welstand requirements when designing his own house in a polder in Amstelveen. The local council wanted the new house to have a traditional roof that met the facade at an angle of between 15 and 60 degrees.

Murphy designed a house where both ground floor and upper floor have tilting walls of glass and sprayed concrete. This way it satisfies the demand for a sloping roof yet looks the very opposite of a faux farmhouse.

Flexible Housing

(Gewild Wonen) Almere

Marlies Rohmer 2001

For her contribution to the building expo 'Gewild Wonen' in Almere-Buiten Marlies Rohmer originally had camper van homes in mind. These were to have consisted of a fixed core of WC, bathroom, storage room and kitchen to which a camper van or mobile home could be hitched. This would give the occupants maximum flexibility and mobility. When this idea proved impracticable, Rohmer decided to attach to the fixed core lofty halls that could be subdivided at the future occupants' discretion. This too was abandoned. In the end the client, the Almere-based housing corporation Groene Stad, fixed the interior layout before the homes went on sale. So their future occupants had no say in this at all.
According to Rohmer, the Netherlands of 2001 was not ready for the deregulated housing of Wilde Wonen or even for the freedom of Gewild Wonen. 'Building is a complicated business with a lot of parties involved: contractors, property developers, real estate agents and architects', she said: 'That makes communication difficult. So buyers need guidance. This is something the government could still be doing. But even then Wilde Wonen isn't a solution for mass housing. The steep cost of plots in the Netherlands is in itself prohibitive to all but the extremely well-off. And these have always enjoyed their own form of Wilde Wonen.'

Catalogue Home

Since 1997

When BNA chairman Carel Weeber launched Wilde Wonen in 1997 many feared that the entire country would then suffer from 'white mould'. The white free-standing self-build houses then mainly afflicting the rims of cities and villages in the provinces of Friesland and Groningen would makes inroads into the Randstad conurbation in the west. Some critics expected that 'living wild' would lead to a chaos of houses in all shapes, sizes and styles. Neither of these things happened. In those parts of Vinex settlements set aside for self-build plots most buyers turned out to prefer neo-traditionalist catalogue houses such as faux farmhouses and 1930s-style villas. And in the overriding majority of cases these have external walls of dark brown brick and black roof tiles. The expected white mould had morphed into a black fungus.

Self-build

Enschede

Pi de Bruijn (supervisor) 2003–

In the spring of 2000 much of the Roombeek area of Enschede was obliterated when a fireworks factory exploded. Pi de Bruijn was enlisted to draw up a reconstruction programme. In consultation with the area's inhabitants De Bruijn opted to restore the original street pattern with certain grand additions including three principal axes. Private patronage was given free rein in Nieuw Roombeek; 400 of the 1,500 housing units were privately built.
That said, the self-build in Roombeek is not entirely deregulated. Particularly along the principal axes the unbroken rows of 'townhouses' have to comply with a whole host of regulations. Enschede is the only other city besides Almere where private patronage, to give Wilde Wonen its official name, took off in a big way. Since 2008, other cities including Amsterdam have been issuing plots for self-builders, partly as a result of the housing crisis. With limited success, however, the biggest stumbling block being the sky-high price of land.

Villa SR Rijssen

Reitsema & Partners 2013

Architect Carel Weeber once compared architecture to clothes. There you have traditional costumes, uniforms, ready-to-wear clothes and haute couture. Traditional costumes in housing are old farmhouses and canal houses. Haute couture covers the one-offs like museums. 'In the Netherlands housing is still at the uniform stage', he explained: 'The Vinex settlements look like the Red Army used to look during a May Day Parade in Moscow's Red Square. In housing we must go for ready-to-wear. Ready-to-wear clothes, from Prada to clothes supermarkets like Zeeman, give everyone, rich and poor, the feeling that they are doing the choosing.' One more category needs adding to Weeber's list: the made-to-measure suit. Take Villa SR in Rijssen in the east of the country. Originally its client wanted a house of 350 square metres for a fairly modest budget. But the architect, Reitsema & Partners, managed to convince him that he could better use his budget to get onto site an elegant, made-to-measure house of 160 square metres instead.

Institute for Sound and Vision

Hilversum

Neutelings Riedijk Architects

2006

Just as postmodernism had been written off on more than one occasion, for the past decade we have been hearing that icons, as striking, often sculptural buildings are called, have had their day. In 2012 the chief message at the 13th Architecture Biennale in Venice, entitled 'Common Ground', was that the age of icons was over.
A year later a number of young Dutch architects including ZUS en DUS Architects made the same claim. And the *Architecture in the Netherlands Yearbook 2012/13* described iconic architecture as a phenomenon rendered obsolete by the change in Zeitgeist.
But the predicted end is a long time coming. Of course the number of spectacular buildings will decrease in light of what would now seem to be a long-term reduction in building since the onset of the economic crisis in 2008. Even so, the future will from time to time bring us city halls, museums and other haute couture buildings such as this Institute for Sound and Vision.

An Architecture of Spectacle

Chapter 10

An often heard complaint at the onset of the twenty-first century was that there were far too many icons being built. Since the swirling, gleaming Guggenheim Museum (1997) designed by American architect Frank Gehry in Bilboa demonstrated that an 'icon' can change an industrial city in decline into a tourist hotspot, so many have been built throughout the world that they have become a problem. If everything is odd, the icons' critics reason, odd becomes normal. Then even the most spectacular building fails to stand out and ceases to be an icon.

Ironically it was Rem Koolhaas, designer of the biggest and most famous icon of the new millennium, the CCTV headquarters in Beijing, who in 2007 exhorted clients and architects to put an end to 'iconic architecture'. In vain, needless to say, since icons are of all times. The difference is that landmark buildings of the past, such as medieval Gothic cathedrals, seventeenth-century royal palaces and nineteenth-century railway stations, were not known as icons. It is only in the past 15 years or so that eye-catching buildings have been given that name.

That said, more icons have been built in recent decades than ever before. There is a simple reason for this proliferation: the years 1990–2008 were a time of unprecedented worldwide prosperity. While the West experienced a relatively strong economic growth, giants like China, India and, ultimately, Brazil awoke from their economic sleep and developed at a furious rate. In China fishing villages changed within 15 years into metropolises and in the United Arab Emirates entire forests of icons sprang up in what had been desert. And just as those in power in the capitalist West had been commissioning icons to express that power for centuries, now Indian industrial magnates, Arab oil sheiks and Chinese state institutions want to erect buildings they can use as logos.

Architects are all too willing to address the worldwide need for icons. After all, they are a way of spreading their fame. They know that well-crafted but unobtrusive buildings are not going to get them into the architectural magazines and onto the websites in this age of mass media. So everyone, supplier and customer alike, benefits from icons: a society of spectacle calls for an architecture of spectacle and gets it from architects who specialize in spectacle.

The Netherlands itself basked in economic prosperity from 1985 to 2008 and has built icons of its own to show for it. The most effective form for these, and therefore the one most used, was the mega sculpture. At times these were sullen and leaden like the earthy Minnaert Building designed by Neutelings Riedijk in Utrecht (1997), at others smooth and buoyant like Meyer en Van Schooten's hovering ING Bank headquarters in Amsterdam (2002). And at other times still they were not only exuberant form-wise but eye-poppingly colourful to boot, such as UNStudio's bright orange theatre in Lelystad (2007).

One of the first sculptural buildings in this country was Piraeus, the massive dark-coloured housing block of 1994 designed by the German architects Hans Kollhoff and Christian Rapp on a tongue of land in Amsterdam's eastern docks area. It is a sculpture with a cause: Piraeus's gently raked form was prompted by a little old harbour office, a listed building that was to stay put. Kollhoff and Rapp draped their colossus around it. That aside, Kollhoff has admitted that the form in general was inspired by the expressionism of the Amsterdam School.

The Piraeus building is the most influential building in Dutch architecture of the past 20 years. It not only signalled the onset of the long-term vogue for dark brick external walls, but elevated Kollhoff and Rapp's neo-expressionism to a popular trend. Sculptural buildings, often sculptural for no good reason, sprang up all over the Netherlands. An Amsterdam example is Jeanne Dekkers' gigantic brick boulder of 2006 housing the Training Institute for Health and Welfare (OZW).

Like contemporary retro buildings, there is a formula for sculptural buildings: take a box, make some incisions in it or even a hole, tack on some appurtenances and hey presto: your neo-expressionist building is ready.

The pioneers of this neo-expressionism were Willem Jan Neutelings and Michiel Riedijk. Their residential tower block (1994) on the dam leading to Java-eiland in Amsterdam was worked up with a few simple recesses and cantilevers into a 'rough volume, as stark as a harbour silo', as they themselves describe it in their book *At Work* (2004).

In this book Neutelings and Riedijk make a serious attempt to give their neo-expressionism a theory. Their architecture rests on three pillars, they explain: knowledge, skill and evocation, a triumvirate that recalls that of the Roman architect Vitruvius: firmness, commodity and delight. Evocation can be regarded as a modern version of delight or *venustas*, a concept that vanished from architectural theory during the twentieth century: 'orchestrating mental images, organizing inspiration so as to make meaningful buildings'.

The first chapter of *At Work* is called 'Sculpture'. 'Buildings are sculptures in the city,' they write: 'Each has its own character, they may be grumpy, happy, dull or serious. They may be short and slight or broad-shouldered. They have a torso, a back, a head or a tail. Accordingly, we work like sculptors: a building needs to be carved slowly, wrested from the polystyrene blocks in our model room.'

But it's never just about form in Neutelings and Riedijk's sculptural architecture. It was for good reason that they were included among the SuperDutch architects in 2000: almost all their buildings step off from an underlying idea, a 'concept' that determines that building's form. 'We give the client what they want, but not what they expect', Willem Jan Neutelings once said. In the Minnaert Building, for example, it is the idea of combining corridors, stairs and other undifferentiated space ('tare space' as they call it) into a large hall. Ranged around this, connected to it with a minimum of stairs and corridors, are the practical classrooms, lecture rooms and offices. So the Minnaert Building gained a large common space that had not been on the clients' wish list at all.

The rise of neo-expressionism in Dutch architecture was paralleled by the sensational reappearance of decoration. This was another area in which Neutelings and Riedijk were pioneers. They were among the first non-traditionalist architects to chip away at the taboo on ornaments, which had persisted longer in the Netherlands than in other Western countries due to the mass conversion of young architects to neo-modernism in the second half of the 1980s. The veins on the Minnaert Building are an early example of decoration in contemporary Dutch architecture. In 2006 there was the Institute for Sound and Vision in Hilversum with its multicoloured cladding panels bearing in relief 'iconic' images from the history of Dutch television. They went a step further the following year in the Walter Bos Complex, the extension to the Central Tax Office in Apeldoorn. Here they commissioned artist Rob Birza to design grotesque beasts on the metal frontage, like gargoyles on a Gothic cathedral.

For most other neo-expressionists the return of decoration was more gradual than it had been for Neutelings and Riedijk. The first embellishments to appear on modern Dutch buildings were cautious in the extreme, preferably in the form of glass facades with depictions of leaves or abstract patterns in or on the glass. Frits van Dongen, for example, had the glass cladding panels of the Philharmonie (2005), Haarlem's concert hall, printed with a graphic depiction of music by the Dutch composer Louis Andriessen. This was the best of both worlds: the facade remained taut and smooth as in modernism yet was decorated, be it with neat abstract patterns.

The next step in the new decorativeness was a cladding of relief panels, exemplified by the cast-iron panels of Rotterdam's Schiecentrale, converted in 2007 by Mei Architects. Here, as in most other reliefs on exterior walls from that time, animals, wheels, ships and other objects are shallowly impressed in the iron, so that they are poorly visible from a distance and seem to form abstract patterns. During the past five years, however, Dutch architects have become steadily bolder and the reliefs deeper and more numerous. The Jatopa housing complex (2009), a product of urban restructuring by Köther Salman Koedijk Architecten in Amsterdam's Nieuw-West quarter, is even clad throughout its height with concrete panels covered with animals, plants, helicopters, wheels and other artefacts in clearly visible relief designed by Studio Job. All kinds of brickwork bonds, much favoured by the expressionists of the Amsterdam School at the start of the twentieth century, also came back into vogue.

Thus we see Dutch architects in the years around 2007 flagrantly and collectively violating the ban on decoration in architecture, exactly a century after the Austrian architect Adolf Loos had imposed it in his infamous essay 'Ornament and Crime'.

The Rock Amsterdam

Erick van Egeraat 2007

Repeating the strategy followed at Kop van Zuid in Rotterdam, foreign architects of repute were invited to build towers on Amsterdam's Zuidas (literally, southern axis), the Netherlands' most up-market office area. And just as at Kop van Zuid the foreigners, amongst whom Pritzker Prize winner Toyo Ito (JP), Norman Foster (GB) and Rafael Moneo (US), have not produced their best work at Zuidas. Far and away the most 'iconic' building at Zuidas is The Rock, designed by Erick van Egeraat. The tower certainly lives up to its name: a rugged, rocky crown sitting atop a glass base. The interior, boasting un-Dutch quantities of cut stone, is equally opulent. For all that, The Rock is a 'sustainable' building that has been awarded the international Carbon Verified certificate. According to Van Egeraat wealth and sustainability are not mutually exclusive, quite the opposite in fact. Of The Rock he said, 'I'm convinced that fine details generate more than they cost. Things like natural stone floors and walls have great staying power. Buildings with a personality are changed less quickly than anonymous architecture and therefore possess an aesthetic sustainability.'

De Sfinxen Huizen

Neutelings Riedijk Architects

2003

When Willem Jan Neutelings informed the audience during his celebrated lecture at the 'Architectuur 2.0' symposium at De Doelen concert hall in Rotterdam in 2007 that the future would not be about spectacle buildings like museums but about the background (he used the word 'fond'), the 95 per cent of everyday buildings, some critics responded with a *tu quoque*. Weren't Neutelings and Riedijk themselves the pre-eminent architects of eccentric buildings? Hadn't they themselves stated in their book *At Work* (2004) that buildings should be landmarks in the city and that this could be achieved by designing them as sculptures? Indeed, as pioneers of neo-expressionism Willem Jan Neutelings and Michiel Riedijk are advocates of 'architecture parlante'. Accordingly, they designed the 152 residential units in the waters of Gooimeer as five sphinx-like sculptural monoliths standing guard along the coast of Huizen. That said, they don't feel that every building should be a landmark, despite what their critics claim. In an interview, they gave to understand that architects should only make landmarks when the brief and context require it.

ING House Amsterdam

Meyer en Van Schooten 2002

ING House, the new head office of the ING Bank, had several nicknames to its credit even before it had been completed. 'Bottle bank', 'clap skate', 'ski boot', 'loot boot' and 'hand vac' were the names (or rather their English equivalents) given to the glass building on stilts. The evening news on TV added another on the day ING House was taken into use: glass slipper. But of course this was much too refined to stick as a nickname.
Which names does that leave? Bottle bank is the first to go as the shape is wrong and the glass aspect is hardly unique for a building. Ski boot is equally inapplicable – ski boots are taller. A clap skate doesn't describe ING House either: there's no iron blade and too many points of support. That leaves us with loot boot and hand vac. And the winner is hand vac. Not just because this nickname passes comment on the nature of a bank group (the Dutch *kruimeldief*, as a hand vac is often called in the Netherlands, literally translates as 'crumb-thief'!) but also because the new building bears a remarkable resemblance to the new generation of hand-held vacuums. The Black & Decker Wet & Dry ('a cordless hand vac that picks up both wet and dry messes') with its streamlined form and transparent portion could almost be ING House in miniature.

Walter Bos Complex Apeldoorn

Neutelings Riedijk Architects and DP6 2007

Neutelings and Riedijk choose different artists and graphic designers to provide the decoration for each of their buildings. One is Jaap Drupsteen who designed the multicoloured glass cladding panels of the Institute for Sound and Vision featuring images from Dutch television history in relief. The 3,000 hands gracing the Museum on the River (MAS, 2010) in Antwerp were the work of the Belgian Tom Hautekiet.
For their part of the Walter Bos office complex for the Central Tax Office in Apeldoorn Neutelings and Riedijk invited the artist Rob Birza to design the decoration. Birza's contributions include the dragon's heads on the mastabas rising from pools on the roof that act as light scoops for the offices below. Like the archives of the Institute for Sound and Vision a large share of the offices is below ground level. As for the similarities between the two buildings, Michiel Riedijk once said, 'We architects should count ourselves lucky if we have one or two decent ideas during our career.'

De Matrix Hardenberg

Marlies Rohmer 2007

De Matrix, an extended school designed in Hardenberg by Marlies Rohmer, brings to mind the houses in Los Angeles of Frank Lloyd Wright. The school's facades of fibre-glass reinforced polyester coffers resemble the decorated textile blocks cladding Wright's Ennis House of 1923 from top to bottom.
In 2012 Rohmer did something architects almost never do. She made a tour of all the buildings she had designed during her 25-year career to see how they had fared. She was reasonably happy about her later work but her early work was a different matter. Her visit to Bleijenburg (1993), a student house in the centre of The Hague, left her 'shocked and disappointed'. 'It is an old building, of course', she admitted. 'I wanted to make it a sculpture that slotted well into the city. The brickwork has aged reasonably well. But the ground floor looks shabby, with those wooden frames and empty workspaces.'

Extension and Renovation of the Stedelijk Museum

Amsterdam

Benthem Crouwel Architekten

2012

It took all of 12 years to find and see onto site a buildable design for the extension to Amsterdam's Stedelijk Museum. Back in 1992 the then new museum director had ditched his predecessor's choice of design by the postmodernists Robert Venturi and Denise Scott Brown. Then his own favourite, the Portuguese Alvaro Siza, spent years in the clinch with the so-called 'donkey's ear' (*Ezelsoor*), a sloping patch of lawn above parking and a supermarket that had miraculously appeared when the surrounding Museumplein was being reconfigured.

When that director left in 2003, the Stedelijk Museum ended its relationship with Siza. His design would have been too expensive, it was claimed, and failed to meet the demands made by the museum. In a new invited competition the jury chose a truly iconic design by Benthem Crouwel. Their extension to the Stedelijk Museum took the form of a gigantic white bathtub.

It was slow going getting the tub on site. First the building contractor went bankrupt and the cladding panels languished in some remote part of the country. The second contractor soon made it known that they would need more time and that the building was going to cost an additional 4.5 million euros. When the new build was finally on site, twenty years after the first design, the American architecture critic Michael Kimmelman wrote in *The New York Times*: 'Offhand I can't recall seeing a more ridiculous looking building than the new Stedelijk Museum. Entering an oversize plumbing fixture to commune with classic modern art is like hearing Bach played by a man wearing a clown suit.'

University Library Utrecht

Wiel Arets 2004

The principal building of Wiel Arets' library for Utrecht University in De Uithof is a large box. The black concrete cladding is for the book depots, with glazing for all other facilities. The depots hang in the box like 'concrete clouds' (the architect's description). Between and below the clouds are the public zones in all shapes and sizes.
The university library is one of an increasing number of early twenty-first century buildings to be decorated. Its glazing is printed with a Kim Zwarts photograph of willows, a species of tree heavily represented in the polder landscape around the campus. The concrete bears the same willow branch motif in relief.

Agora Lelystad

UNStudio/Ben van Berkel 2007

The Agora theatre and convention centre in Lelystad is everything Almere's Kunstlinie theatre of earlier that year is not. If the Kunstlinie, the work of the Japanese SANAA practice, is an assemblage of unobtrusive grey boxes, the Agora, designed by Ben van Berkel of UNStudio, is a bona fide landmark in the city. This is not just because of its angular, sculptural forms but more particularly because its blistering orange exterior is visible from afar. Orange was a fashionable colour in Dutch architecture during the 2000s.
In 2001, the dazzling orange studio house of the Thonik graphic design practice, built to a design by MVRDV in the courtyard of a housing block in Amsterdam, caused a minor riot. Local residents objected to the colour, which they claimed was literally painful to behold. The matter was resolved by painting the building bright green.
The orange of the Agora theatre is too much of a good thing as well. True, iconic architecture is appropriate for a theatre but the combination of the over-the-top orange colour with the skewed crystalline forms carries it into the realm of avant-garde kitsch.

Central Station

Rotterdam

Benthem Crouwel Architekten, West 8 and Meyer en Van Schooten architecten 2013

The new Central Station in Rotterdam is another building to earn itself a nickname before it was completed. This was 'de puntzak', after the triangular paper bag used to serve up French fries. 'Shark's mouth' is another.
The new Central Station, built in connection with the construction of the HSL high speed rail link, replaces the railway station of 1957 designed by Sybold van Ravensteyn. The main concourse of the original station had a magnificent roof of undulating concrete shells. As if to outdo Van Ravensteyn, the team of architects responsible for the new building designed the entire concourse as a single gigantic wave. The cladding on the inside of the wave is timber, that of the exterior stainless steel. Rotterdam Central Station is one building that demonstrates that even the neo-functionalists Jan Benthem and Mels Crouwel now make neo-expressionist sculptures. Their gigantic bathtub of an extension to the Stedelijk Museum in Amsterdam opened in 2012.

STATION

Thermal Power Plant Utrecht

Liesbeth van der Pol 2005

During the golden years of Dutch architecture it wasn't only haute couture buildings like museums that were icons. Even industrial and public utility buildings such as pumping stations and bridgemaster's houses were given arresting forms. This invites parallels with the halcyon days of the Amsterdam School, when everyday artefacts like waste bins and electrical substations were subjected to the coercion of expressionist form.

Sited in De Uithof, this thermal power plant is a neo-expressionist sculpture. Perhaps neo-futurist is a more apt description. For Liesbeth van der Pol's Corten steel enveloped energy plant is an ode to the fantastic designs for energy plants and stations by the Italian Futurist Antonio Sant'Elia.

Kraton 230 Rotterdam

Mei Architects 2007

The re-emergence of ornament in Dutch architecture is readily apparent on Lloydpier in Rotterdam. Here in the years centring on 2000 several buildings once serving the Schiecentrale, a now disused electricity generating plant, were converted into premises for offices, apartments and hospitality. If 25kV, the first building to be refurbished to a design by Mei Architects, now boasts a sleek new glass front, Kraton 230, completed in 2007, is clad in Corten steel panels with decorations in relief. You have to get close to the building to see that the panels, designed by Studio Job, bear depictions of ships, cogwheels, whales and other things related to the docks and water.
Mei Architects have resorted to decoration in other buildings too. 'Attention, that's what it's about', said Robert Winkel of Mei Architects in an interview about a garage in Almere he had decorated: 'Everyone likes to get attention. But we Dutch don't invest much love in our buildings. We're too Calvinist, too strait-laced, too stingy. Look, everywhere in this country you see that same shabby modernist crap. I wanted to make something that radiates attention and joy, something that belongs here.'

Jatopa Amsterdam

Köther Salman Koedijk Architecten 2009

The objections to decoration that the Austrian architect Adolf Loos expressed in his famous essay 'Ornament and Crime' of 1907 were mainly moral ones. Who, Loos asked his readers, have tattoos on their bodies? The answer being primitive peoples and criminals. 'The modern man who tattoos himself is either a criminal or a degenerate,' he wrote. It was a sign of refinement to leave bodies and buildings undecorated.
In the Netherlands decoration remained a taboo in architecture longer than in many other countries. This was because Dutch architecture was still heavily moralist in the 1980s and 1990s, not least due to the tirades of Aldo van Eyck. A century on from 'Ornament and Crime', however, that moralism has largely dissipated here too and decoration in architecture is back. You can see it in the Jatopa housing project in Overtoomse Veld in Amsterdam's Nieuw-West quarter. Here no less than 800 square metres of decorated concrete panels have been worked into the facade. The decorations in relief (animals, wheels, helicopters and other artefacts) were designed by Studio Job.

EYE Amsterdam

Delugan Meissl Associated Architects 2012

There is no escaping the comparison: EYE, the new film institute in Amsterdam is the little brother of the Sydney Opera House. Like Jørn Utzon's world-famous building EYE, designed by the Austrian architects Roman Delugan and Elke Meissl, enjoys a prominent place on the waterfront. Both are sterling examples of spectacle architecture that recall forms of animal life. If the opera house resembles a pair of amorous turtles, EYE looks like a grasshopper, particularly when viewed from the ferry crossing the IJ inlet between Centraal Station and the north of the city (Amsterdam-Noord).
Both buildings are wonderfully massed and sited at the water's edge. And the comparison doesn't end there. If the Sydney Opera House has burgeoned into the icon of that city if not of Australia as a whole, EYE has the potential of becoming the symbol of Amsterdam-Noord and maybe of all Amsterdam.

De Rotterdam Rotterdam

OMA/Rem Koolhaas 2013

When buildings turn out very large, it creates a problem, as Rem Koolhaas explained in 1993 in his article 'Bigness or the Problem of Large'. 'The "art" of architecture', he contended, 'is useless in Bigness.'
About the same time he was writing 'Bigness' Koolhaas and his Office for Metropolitan Architecture (OMA) made the design for De Rotterdam at Kop van Zuid in the Rotterdam docklands. It took nearly 20 years for construction of the towers to get under way. But they got built in the end, during the economic crisis too; this hit the Dutch building industry particularly hard.
It was help from the city council that enabled De Rotterdam to get built. To encourage the building's developers to act, the council promised to rent a large part of it as office space for its officials. It seemed unconcerned that this would mean emptying two of the three towers of Europoint (1975), designed by Skidmore, Owings & Merrill. Building De Rotterdam was, in effect, building for vacancy.
De Rotterdam has been called the Netherlands' biggest mixed-use building. And yet its bigness was not really a problem for Koolhaas at the end of the day: he simply applied the 'art of architecture' in the design. The look of the colossal new city icon towering above that other icon, the Erasmus Bridge, was dictated by a simple 'architectural gesture': three 150-metre-high towers with skewed, jutting upper portions standing atop a six-storey concrete base the size of a football pitch. The towers huddle so closely together that from many vantage points they present a single gigantic wall of glass and aluminium.

Market Hall Rotterdam

MVRDV 2014

In the closing decades of the twentieth century many dilapidated nineteenth-century market halls in European cities embarked on a new life. The market halls of London's Covent Garden, for example, after briefly closing in the 1970s, grew into a major tourist attraction. Indeed, when the urban middle class showed an increasing interest in 'good' food after century's end, many new market halls were built in European cities.

One such city was Rotterdam, which, with an eye to making its centre more attractive to the middle class, wanted a market hall of its own. So ten years ago the city council held a competition to design a 'market building', a combination of market hall and apartments. MVRDV won with a fusion of housing and hall: the 228 rented and freehold apartments constitute the walls as well as the roof of the Market Hall.

'This was the one way to make the Market Hall a large indoor urban space', explained MVRDV front man Winy Maas: 'Many of our designs are about intensive, ultra dense development. But you have to counter this with space. You can compare the hall with the churches in the older parts of Rome. They also act as squares, if you like, public halls in the middle of a sea of houses. The Market Hall has become a cathedral with housing inside it.'

This is a building of vast dimensions and numbers. It has a total surface area of 96,000 square metres. The hall has been sunk 15 metres into the boggy ground and is 40 metres high. Front and rear have all-glass areas that extend almost the entire height. The gigantic barrel vault is decorated with *Cornucopia*, an artwork with a surface area of 11,000 square metres designed by Arno Coenen and Iris Roskam. Gigantic strawberries, snow peas, avocados, cows, lilies and butterflies, digitally projected onto 4,000 aluminium panels of 1.5 x 1.5 metres, seem to rain down like manna from heaven.

Extension to Museum de Fundatie Zwolle

Bierman Henket architecten

2012

Just how strong the temptation is to design an 'icon' in the age of spectacle architecture is evident from this extension to Museum de Fundatie in Zwolle. Hubert-Jan Henket, jointly responsible for the new build portion atop the former Palace of Justice (1841) designed by Eduard Louis de Coninck, has always strongly opposed spectacle architecture. He regards himself as an heir to the Modern Movement and considers its 'spiritual economy' to be as relevant as ever. 'We derive form from function and technique, from material properties that we exploit to the full', he said in an interview in 2001. 'That's why we set out to discard every form of decoration so as to make something that's as balanced and as functional as possible.'

So it came as quite a surprise when Henket's extension to De Fundatie turned out to be a thoroughly unfunctional blob. Not only is a blob full of unusable reserve space but it is also unpractical as a place for exhibiting art works. Moreover, this blob has been embellished with a cladding of ceramic tiles from the Tichelaar works in a decorative pattern. The new extension to the Zwolle museum is a far cry indeed from the 'spiritual economy' that Henket has advocated throughout his career.

Bollenveld Den Bosch
Dries Kreijkamp 1984

The 50 globe dwellings in Den Bosch date from a time when sustainable building was, at least in this country, still called environmentally friendly or green building and was mainly about energy-saving. In fact, this last-named aspect was what enabled artist Dries Kreijkamp to get his globe dwellings onto site. His argument was that the sphere had the smallest surface area of all three-dimensional forms.
This inhabitable version of the locally made 'chocolate ball' (Bossche bol) was not built the way Kreijkamp had intended, the globes being executed in concrete instead of polyester. Soon enough the dwellings were plagued with flaws of all kinds which made them much more expensive to build than Kreijkamp had hoped.
Since then, sustainable building has grown into a virtually all-inclusive phenomenon in architecture. These days it also relates to demolition, the choice and handling of materials, the actual building process and the environment inside the built result. In recent years it has transpired that sustainability is also a question of aesthetics: buildings that look good are less likely to be demolished.

A Return to Craft Skills

Chapter 11

Visit the site of any Dutch architecture firm and it is almost certain to tell you that sustainable building is an important aspect of that firm's work. Certainly since 2006, when the former US vice-president Al Gore made the film *An Inconvenient Truth* about the consequence of global warming, every architect sees sustainable building as a necessity.

Although sustainable building only really became general practice in the Netherlands round about 1990, it had already had quite a history by then. Functionalism, which first emerged in the 1920s, is in a sense itself already a form of sustainable building. Unlike now, this was less a question of saving energy or reducing carbon emissions than of using a minimum of building materials. Armed with the maxim 'form follows function' the functionalists sought to design buildings that were tailored to their purpose as precisely and efficiently as possible. They regarded decoration as a waste of material, money and labour. They also preferred flat roofs because they required less material than traditional pitched roofs.

It was after the 1972 report by the Club of Rome about the finite nature of the supply of raw materials and the first oil crisis in 1973, which caused energy prices to soar, that the accent in sustainable building shifted to energy-saving. This not only meant that the Dutch population was called upon to break with the tradition of leaving the curtains open at night but also that the government imposed an increasing number of rules relating to the insulation and energy-saving capacities of buildings. Lastly, all these measures were set down in the first Building Decree of 1992. The second decree in 2003 contained still more provisions for energy-saving, such as the Energy Performance Coefficient to which buildings now have to adhere.

The authorities have also promoted sustainable building with subsidies. For example Bollenveld (1984), a settlement in Den Bosch of globe dwellings designed by Dries Kreijkamp, was subsidized by the local council because these homes were assumed to be 'energy-efficient, environmentally friendly, low-cost and low-maintenance'. This proved to be an error of judgement. The globes were plagued with humidity problems and as early as 2004, 20 years after being built, were given a thorough overhaul and a new, waterproof skin.

The globe dwellings date from the time when sustainable building was still known as 'green building' and was mainly the province of idealistic architects like Kreijkamp. Their idealism is often expressed in a literally green architecture with grass roofs and lots of wood. The tendency to make green buildings green persists even today. 2012Architecten (now Superuse Studios), a practice that regards sustainability as a priority, has specialized in buildings that ostentatiously use surplus materials. A good example is Villa Welpeloo in Enschede (2010), built almost entirely of waste materials including outer walls of wood that would otherwise be used for burning.

Yet even in the 1990s, when green building was promoted to sustainable building, it was clear that environmentally friendly architecture was not necessarily informed by a green aesthetic. Sustainability proved largely to be a question of technical installations; the architecture itself could take a wide variety of forms. Ruurd Roorda's extension to a tax office building in Enschede (1996), for example, stylistically is more neo-modernist than green, but is nonetheless exceedingly energy-efficient thanks to a heavy concrete core that collects heat during the day and releases it at night. And the work of Paul de Ruiter, an architect who throughout his career has been seriously interested in sustainability, demonstrates that super-sleek high-tech buildings can be energy-efficient.

In the 1990s sustainability proved to be not just a question of eco friendliness. With the renewal of the post-war residential areas inevitably came the awareness that housing built to 'sustainable', functionalist principles was first in line for the wrecker's ball. Just that fitness for purpose had rendered non-sustainable these 'dwellings for the *existenzminimum*', as the German architects of the Neue Sachlichkeit of the 1920s described their workers' housing. Half a century ago, many homes in reconstruction-era estates had been built to accept what was then the core family of two adults and two children but around 2000 they no longer met occupant requirements, which had changed dramatically, largely owing to the increase in prosperity and advances in technology. Add to this the fact that after 50 years these economical dwellings built with cheap materials had often reached the end of their useful life. To compound matters, their standardized production with precast concrete panels made them inflexible and difficult to alter. In many cases renovation would have been more expensive than new build and demolition. And demolition, as all eco builders will tell you, is the industry's least sustainable solution.

The wholesale demolition of minimalist, economical homes caused some housebuilders such as Frank Bijdendijk, director of the Amsterdam housing corporation Het Oosten (since 2008 one half of Stadgenoot), to conclude that it was capacious buildings with a solid frame that were sustainable. A loose-fit format would allow flexibility of use and make the buildings easy to adapt to meet whatever demands might be made of them in the near or distant future.

In his call for erecting spacious buildings with solid frames meant to last for ever, Bijdendijk always presented the traditional Amsterdam canal house as the epitome of sustainability. The roomy seventeenth-century residences and warehouses have had many different duties to perform over the years. If they were often used in the 1970s for offices, these days they can be reconverted into houses with little difficulty.

In the early years of the twenty-first century, Stadgenoot commissioned a couple of Solids in Amsterdam as examples of sustainable live-work buildings. Solids are large, sturdy buildings whose tall storeys allow for a flexibility of use. Sustainability in use is not related to a particular architectural style. If the Solid in IJburg, the Amsterdam Vinex development, is a bona fide neoclassical building by the Austrian firm of Baumschlager Eberle, that in Amsterdam-West by UK architect Tony Fretton is a no-frills combination of brick and glass architecture as often come across in Dutch urban restructuring areas.

The mass demolition of housing units in the urban restructuring areas brought with it the discovery that sustainability had a third side to it: aesthetics. The bare, no-nonsense houses of the reconstruction era proved remarkably unpopular: there was less resistance to demolishing these than there had been to the nineteenth-century areas twenty years previously. No one except architectural historians and a handful of architecturally enlightened residents mourned the loss of the clapped-out 'minimum existence' housing. Thus, urban regeneration made clear that in terms of architectural taste there was now a yawning chasm between designers and experts in architecture and the man or woman in the street. FARO Architects, designers of many urban regeneration projects, carried out a number of studies into this disparity in taste, with surprising results.

When organizing the 'test of taste' in 2007 FARO architect Jurgen van der Ploeg presumed that most laypersons preferred traditionalist architecture and that architects, critics, housing association officials and other professionals were for modernism. The test, in which 8500 professionals and laypersons were asked to grade 100 wide-ranging examples of Dutch domestic architecture, proved him right: the non-professionals rated traditionalist houses more highly than the professionals.

But it also transpired that the disparity in taste was not as big as FARO had expected: laypersons and professionals had a lot in common. For example, both groups gave high scores to the seventeenth-century rings of canals in Amsterdam and Michel de Klerk's 'Ship' (1920), the most famous example of Amsterdam School architecture. And as for contemporary architecture everyone, professionals as well as non-professionals, showed a preference for neo-expressionism: Neutelings Riedijk's sculptural housing in Huizen scored high among laypersons and professionals alike. Both groups also preferred 'modern retro' to 'historical retro'.

They shared their dislikes as well. Both groups gave their lowest scores to the shabby, unembellished dwellings of around 1980, the age of cauliflower estates and watered-down structuralism. From this FARO concluded that details were overridingly important in evaluating architecture: buildings visibly designed with care and attention came in for high scores.

The survey's conclusion that fine details were of great importance when evaluating a building was consistent with the renewed concern for craft skills among many Dutch architects in the 2010s. In 2009 Michiel Riedijk had organized a series of lectures by international architects entitled 'Architecture as a Craft'; these were later compiled in a book of that name. Earlier, in 2007, his work partner Willem Jan Neutelings had caused a stir at the symposium 'Architectuur 2.0', where Rem Koolhaas, Ben van Berkel and other Dutch name architects pondered the future of architecture. Neutelings called for a return to the essentials of this 'ancient, slow-paced profession' and exhorted his colleagues to abandon their ambitions to become journalists, computer wizards and scientists. Knowledge, skill and evocation – these, according to Neutelings, are still at the core of this 'craft profession with a tradition going back 5,000 years'.

House 2.0 Amsterdam

Pieter Weijnen/FARO Architects 2010

House 2.0 is an improved version of a sustainable house that FARO architect Pieter Weijnen designed for himself and his family in the self-build zone of IJburg, the Amsterdam Vinex settlement. House 2.0 was to be energy-neutral. 'Developments in sustainable building are moving fast,' said Weijnen in 2010 about the improvements. 'Actually, much of the knowledge you need comes from countries like Germany and Austria. The Netherlands has some catching up to do in sustainable and energy-efficient building.' A striking aspect of House 2.0 is the charred wood frontage. 'Charred wood is used in traditional Japanese architecture,' Weijnen explained. 'It can survive without maintenance for decades on end.' Many of the energy-efficient features in House 2.0 are not immediately obvious: 'On the sleeping level upstairs the adobe finish is mixed with tiny paraffin capsules that absorb heat during the day and release it at night. This keeps it wonderfully cool.' House 2.0 is also equipped with facilities that have long been part of the repertoire of sustainable building. Rainwater is collected in a tank and used for the toilet and the washing machine. The roof has solar collectors around the edge and a wind turbine.

Rozet Arnhem

Neutelings Riedijk Architects
2013

'We give the client what they want, but not what they expect', Willem Jan Neutelings once said of the buildings designed by his practice. Rozet is one such surprising building. The new cultural centre, which stands in a part of Arnhem city centre that had been devastated during the Second World War, was to be designed as a 'village square', according to the city council's brief. But it has become more of a village street, or rather a 200-metre-long village stair. Those not visiting Rozet for its cultural facilities still have access to the café and roof garden. Rozet is allied to other 'people's palaces' built by Neutelings and Riedijk in the early years of the twenty-first century in the Netherlands and Belgium. Like the Museum on the River (MAS) completed two years earlier in Antwerp, Rozet is a sturdy building full of contrasts. Another similarity is that Rozet, like MAS, is strikingly decorated. Every single one of the staggered elements of sandy concrete ('Arnhem blond' is how the architects describe its colour) of which the facade is comprised is emblazoned with a rosette. Cast in concrete, this decoration, designed by Catalogtree, is based on the Penrose tiling, a geometrical figure discovered by the mathematician and physicist Roger Penrose.

De Keyser Amsterdam

Tom Frantzen 2011

The greatest discovery made by FARO's tests of architectural taste of around 2007, was that laypersons and experts alike had a horror of early 1980s architecture because of the lack of fine details. Tom Frantzen made a similar discovery when designing De Keyser, a new housing block built in Amsterdam on the site of a predecessor. When the client rejected his first conceptual design for De Keyser and asked for something more traditional, he initially felt burdened by it. 'It kept me awake at night', admitted Frantzen in 2011. 'I don't want to be a retro architect. In the end I decided I would make a traditional building in a new way and execute it perfectly.'
He immersed himself in the architecture of housing blocks from around 1900: 'Designing a facade that sits well in an old street is something one just didn't learn at architecture school. The Classical tripartition of the facade into base, upper storeys and cornice and the rhythm, how the windows were positioned, the wall ties, the colours – I analysed all the compositional resources used to design the original building on site and translated them into principles and techniques used today. I had to teach myself how to design along traditional lines. I'm an autodidact where traditionalism is concerned.'

Renovation of the Rijksmuseum Amsterdam

Cruz y Ortiz 2012

One of the reasons given as to why foreign architects of repute seldom if ever design their best work in the Netherlands is 'the Dutch way of doing things'. Large building projects are often long and laborious with a great many players who take ages to reach agreement, the upshot being an architecture of mediocrity and compromise.

'You never know who decides what in this country', complained Antonio Ortiz, one of the two Spanish architects who in 2001 were given the prestigious task of renovating and enlarging Amsterdam's Rijksmuseum. They had to work with not one but three clients: the Government Buildings Agency who owned the building, the Rijksmuseum itself and Amsterdam-Zuid district council. The council's concern was the infamous arcade of 1885 slicing through the museum; after years of bickering this has ultimately retained its duty as a way-through for cyclists.

Not just that, the Spanish architects found themselves working with restoration architect Van Hoogevest and the French interior designer Jean-Michel Wilmotte. From this developed a protracted discussion about the restoration of the entrance area or Voorhal. In the end this hall was almost entirely rebuilt to the original design by Pierre Cuypers.

Cruz deplored this 'Dutch way of doing things' and would have preferred a powerful official to back them up. In the end, though, the Rijksmuseum is an exception to the rule that foreign architects aren't at their best in the Netherlands. The ten-year operation has had stupendous results. Cruz y Ortiz's key intervention – emptying the courtyards of clutter – has finally given the Rijksmuseum an entrance befitting the most important museum in the Netherlands.

De Collectie | The Collection

IJburg Solid

Amsterdam

Baumschlager & Eberle 2011

Frank Bijdendijk, until 2011 director of the Amsterdam housing association Stadgenoot, sought sustainability particularly in the phenomenon of oversize. Back in the 1980s he had discovered that what made a building like Tetterode type foundry in Amsterdam so easy for squatters to convert into accommodation was the fact that it had a solid shell and capacious rooms.
This discovery led 20 years later to the construction of two 'Solids' in Amsterdam, big buildings with a shell built for eternity and tall spaces that could be used for either living or working. Their flexibility means that Solids, unlike so many hard-to-alter 'form follows function' buildings dating from the post-war reconstruction, would not require demolishing after 50 years. The Austrian architects Baumschlager & Eberle have stressed the solidity and permanence of their Solid on IJburg with a classicist design. After Bijdendijk left Stadgenoot, a study carried out by the housing association declared the Solids to be unprofitable, so that no more are to be built in the near future.

GWL Site

Amsterdam

Kees Christiaanse (urban design) 1998

'The Netherlands' first sustainable housing estate' is how the residents' association describes the GWL site, built in the 1990s on what used to be the grounds of the Municipal Water Board in Amsterdam's Staatslieden neighbourhood. Not so. The GWL site may be the first environmentally friendly housing estate to be endowed with the term 'sustainable', but there are much older eco-estates as they were called until the 1990s. One is Ecolonia in Alphen aan den Rijn, which dates from the previous decade.
In Amsterdam some of the old waterworks buildings, including the water tower, were retained. For the new build blocks, to be erected in an open plan layout, the project's urban designer Kees Christiaanse commissioned the architects, amongst whom Neutelings Riedijk and Meyer en Van Schooten, to cram in as many units as possible with their own entrance and garden, which resulted in a panoply of dwelling types. Kitchen gardens nestling between the uniformly red brick clad blocks are an early form of the urban agriculture so much in vogue in recent years.

NMB Head Office Building Amsterdam

Alberts & Van Huut 1987

Flexibility and energy efficiency, two key elements of sustainability, loomed large in Alberts & Van Huut's design for the head offices of the NMB (now ING Bank) in Amsterdam-Zuidoost. The office building additionally resonates with the anthroposophical ideas held by the architects and the bank's then board of directors: not a right angle in sight, just as in the Goetheanum in Dornach, designed in 1928 by Rudolf Steiner, the founder of anthroposophy.
In the reception accorded the architecture of Alberts & Van Huut we are made aware of the difference between the experts' taste in architecture and that of lay enthusiasts. The public at large has the highest regard for the 'monkey rock', as the NMB office has been dubbed. The Gasunie headquarters in Groningen, a similarly organic design by Alberts & Van Huut, was even chosen in a readers' poll held by *Trouw*, a national daily, as the Netherlands' most attractive building. That said, the firm's work generally gets shorter shrift from critics and fellow architects.

Netherlands Institute of Ecology

Wageningen

Claus en Kaan Architecten 2010

In 2012 the Netherlands Institute of Ecology (NIOO-KNAW) was awarded the 'Golden Pyramid', the national award for enlightened patronage, for its new build premises on the campus of Wageningen University. The institute was under an obligation to deliver a sustainable building. Claus en Kaan took as their stepping-off point the 'cradle to cradle' model. This principle, which made the Americans William McDonough and Michael Braungart world-famous in the early 2000s, stipulates that all building materials can be reused or taken up in a continuous natural cycle.

The Institute admits to certain experimental applications of sustainable building. For example, the green roof is used for research into techniques with which plants can generate electricity.

And yet the Netherlands Institute of Ecology lacks the 'green' look. Despite the abundance of wood inside and out, it is first and foremost an impressive glass building in the modernist tradition.

Extension to Tax Office Building
Enschede

Kingma Roorda architecten 1996

In the early days sustainable building was often accompanied by a green aesthetic. 'Green' buildings were made of 'natural' materials and topped off with a grass roof. But in time sustainable building gradually became less green. Take this tax office building extension designed by Klaas Kingma and Ruurd Roorda, which looks like anything but a green building. The architects sought and found energy efficiency principally in the cooling aspect. They knew that cooling rather than heating was the big energy consumer in office buildings. So they endowed this one with a large thermal mass in the form of sturdy concrete floor slabs. This means that it only heats up gradually, while additional natural ventilation cools it off at night.

Rijkswaterstaat Office Building
Middelburg

Paul de Ruiter 2004

Sustainability has been a key objective in the work of Paul de Ruiter ever since he set up his practice in 1994. Yet this is not apparent from looking at his buildings. Even wood, the pre-eminent sign that a building's architect has hit the sustainability trail, is in short supply.
De Ruiter's office building for Rijkswaterstaat (the national water authority) in Middelburg is sustainable in several ways. It is functionally flexible and internally subdivisible in a great many permutations. It can also be easily partitioned off into single offices, which can then be let individually. It is in addition an energy-efficient building and employs the principle of 'active concrete': the upper storey floors are of concrete 30 centimetres thick in which cooling, air conditioning and a flexible power and data system are stored. This precluded the need for lowered ceilings, the curse of so many interiors.

Villa Welpeloo Enschede

2012Architecten 2010

For 2012Architecten, the firm that rechristened itself Superuse Studios on 20 December 2012, sustainability resides most of all in reusing surplus materials and everyday objects. Their Villa Welpeloo in Enschede is almost entirely constructed of waste material. The exact design had not been decided on when work began on the house. Jan Jongert and Jeroen Bergsma of 2012Architecten proceeded from the fact that the house was to be built as much as possible from discarded materials found in and around Enschede. The design was adapted to accommodate whatever material had been found. Another criterion of theirs besides reuse is to try to use the materials as found, with a minimum of reworking.

Villa Welpeloo, built for a couple with a collection of graphic art, has a supporting structure of steel beams from machines used in local textile factories. The wood of the external walls comes from cable reels discarded by Twentsche Kabelfabriek in Haaksbergen.

Restoration of Zonnestraal Hilversum

Wessel de Jonge and Hubert-Jan Henket 2008

The project to restore Zonnestraal Sanatorium, one of the pinnacles of Dutch Modern Architecture, raised the question of what to do with a building that was not meant to be around for ever.
The architect Jan Duiker had designed the sanatorium in the late 1920s as a temporary structure. There was bound to be a cure for tuberculosis before long, he reasoned, and then the building would serve no further purpose. The first of these expectations was fulfilled, but not the second. Zonnestraal became a general hospital. Some parts were refurbished to the point of becoming unrecognizable, others were left to rack and ruin.
Thanks to the efforts of Hubert-Jan Henket and Wessel de Jonge, the founders of Docomomo, the international committee for Documentation and Conservation of Buildings, Sites and Neighbourhoods of the Modern Movement, Zonnestraal was saved and was treated to an exemplary restoration in the early 2000s.

Ministries of the Interior and Justice The Hague

Hans Kollhoff 2012

De Kroon The Hague

Rapp+Rapp 2011

'Originality is not a mark of quality in architecture', according to Hans Kollhoff, the Berlin architect of the influential Piraeus building in Amsterdam, in an interview in 2003: 'That's why I've been turning more and more over the years to the conventions of architecture, to the old typologies of, say, the dwelling-house and the housing block. I'm increasingly taken with the idea of back-to-basics building, and see "appropriateness" as a key quality in architecture today.' Originality was certainly not the first consideration when designing these two towers for the ministries of Justice and the Interior ('JuBi', to use the Dutch acronym) projected in the centre of The Hague on the site of Carel Weeber's demolished housing block De Zwarte Madonna. Kollhoff, who had previously designed buildings in other Dutch cities (Amersfoort, Rotterdam, Maastricht), sought inspiration for his Hague towers in early American skyscrapers. 'Europe has scarcely any tall buildings with the same quality as the classic skyscrapers in New York and Chicago', he explained in the interview about his designs for the JuBi towers. 'Those early skyscrapers rise from the block structure of the urban ground plan. They get slimmer and more filigreed on the way up and ultimately harmonize with the heavens. Gothic Revival was a suitable style for towers like these. Countering this soaring harmony were the taut boxes proposed by European modernists like Walter Gropius and Ludwig Mies van der Rohe. I always interpret this as the European fear of desecrating the tower theme. The towers of Gothic cathedrals – those were our European skyscrapers and they are breathtaking. The Americans dared to turn these cathedral towers into profane buildings, they entered into dialogue with the heavens. Europeans baulked at the idea.'

Refurbishment of City Theatre Haarlem

Erick van Egeraat 2008

Erick van Egeraat, and not Rem Koolhaas, is the Dutch architect whose work has featured the most in the 25 *Architecture in the Netherlands Yearbooks* issued since 1987, or so it transpired when the 2012 *Yearbook* was published.
Van Egeraat himself was a little surprised. 'I thought Claus en Kaan would win', he said at the launch of the 25th *Yearbook*. 'Their minimalism has been pretty much the standard for ages.'
Van Egeraat saw a rosy future for Dutch architecture in 2012: 'I keep hearing all this doom and gloom stuff about the crisis in architecture and building. But I don't feel there's a direct connection between the economy and the ascendancy of architecture. The stylistic freedom in this country is now much greater than it was ten, 20 years ago and architects make much fuller use of the rich resources that architecture possesses. So yes, it's looking good for Dutch architecture right now.'

The New Freedom

Epilogue

'The normalization of Dutch architecture' would have made a good subtitle for *Double Dutch*. So would 'How moralism vanished from Dutch architecture'. The fact is, when Dutch architecture cautiously began its ascendancy in the mid 1980s moralism was still alive and kicking. Many Dutch architects had strict and simple ideas about 'right' and 'wrong', not least thanks to the polemics of Aldo van Eyck, the influential 'conscience of Dutch architecture'. 'Wrong' was everything that even hinted at postmodernism and 'right' was the tradition of the Great Gang, as Van Eyck called the pioneers of modernism. Van Eyck's moralism was founded on a belief in the Zeitgeist. Architects, he felt, had a duty to be 'absolutely modern' and they could only be modern if their work was in chime with that of the Great Gang.

A quarter century later, this moralism has all but disappeared. As Kees van der Hoeven, architect and former chairman of the Union of Dutch Architects, put it in an interview he gave to *NRC Handelsblad* in the summer of 2012, 'One difference between architecture now and 25 years ago is that these days "anything goes".' As co-editor of *Architecture in the Netherlands Yearbook* (2008-2012), he was looking back on the golden quarter century of Dutch architecture: 'There's no taboo or physical restriction on what you can make these days. When I began my career, you didn't even consider polystyrene cladding. Now it's quite normal. But perhaps the most significant change is that there's no longer a taboo on back-to-the-classics architecture. Neo-traditionalism is now pretty well accepted. Sjoerd Soeters has two large historicist projects in the latest *Yearbook* – the city hall in Zaandam and the provincial hall in Leeuwarden. Particularly the Leeuwarden project, in which a truly monumental city block has been almost surgically restored and enlarged, is a stunning piece of work. Stunning it may be but it would never have made it to the *Yearbook* 25 or even ten years ago.'

Even the belief in the Zeitgeist, which prompted the duty to be modern in the first place, has worn thin. Some architects discovered that the spirit of the age speaks 'double Dutch' or is even an *idée fixe* and felt free to build in any number of styles. 'Time makes no demands', said fusion architect Wilfried van Winden in an interview in 2006: 'Or rather: the idea that a spirit of the times dictates things to us is a tautology. There is no spirit of the times. Everything now taking place and being made is of these times. Even the longing for things of the past, not just in architecture but everywhere, is of these times.'

So the Netherlands is no longer the Cuba of international architecture, where the modernist tradition is all-pervading, and Dutch architecture has regained its freedom: 'They're still around, you know,' said Van der Hoeven on the subject of the new freedom, 'modernist architects who refuse to be clubbed together with an architect specializing in the Palladian style, only now they are the exception. In fact these days most Dutch architects are influenced by neo-traditionalism, if unconsciously. We are all much freer than we were a quarter century ago.'

The last years of the liberation of Dutch architecture coincided with the financial-economic crisis that broke in 2008. This hit the Netherlands with terrible and sustained force and had major repercussions for its architecture. The building industry collapsed and half of the 15,000 architects that the Netherlands had in 2007 have since lost their jobs. The infrastructure supporting Dutch architecture has suffered too. In 2013, exactly 20 years after the Netherlands Architecture Institute moved into its own newly built premises, it was closed down and merged with two other organizations as The New Institute, for architecture, design and e-culture. In similar fashion, the Netherlands Architecture Fund was transformed into the Creative Industries Fund NL, which is a good deal less generous with its grants for architects than its predecessor. Even the Berlage Institute ceased to exist as an independent entity and became part of the Faculty of Architecture at Delft University of Technology. In 2010 the Ministry of Housing, Spatial Planning and the Environment (VROM), for decades the driving force behind spatial planning in this country, was dissolved. Spatial planning is now mainly the responsibility of local government bodies. Public housing, once a pillar of the Dutch welfare state, is now left largely to the mercies of the market.

It is no accident that the liberation of Dutch architecture coincided with the age of neoliberalism and the demise of the welfare state. Until the 1990s the state played a key role in public housing and spatial planning. But as the century ended, more and more politicians and administrators began to see state intervention as an obstacle to healthy economic development. As a result the housing corporations were given financial independence as early as 1994. This lost them their dominant position in housing and finally opened the doors to postmodernism in Dutch architecture. The market, after all, was calling for masses of traditionalist architecture and got this from the property developers and building contractors who had taken over domestic construction from the housing corporations.

This was the beginning of the end of what Carel Weeber used to call 'state architecture'. If the older new build estates were almost entirely comprised of subsidized rented dwellings, these only constitute 30 per cent of the housing in the majority of Vinex settlements. The same figure holds for the renewal of post-war areas in the medium-to-large Dutch cities.

It took until 2012 for the curtain to come down on traditional Dutch social housing. In the years ahead the corporations will be hard put to continue building new social housing units, as they made known when Mark Rutte's Second Cabinet, a coalition of Liberals (VVD) and Social Democrats (PvdA), announced that from 2016 the corporations would have to pay tax to the tune of 1.7 billion euros.

If the corporations stick to their guns, this really will be the end, after a century and a half, of Dutch social housing. Of course some corporations will still occasionally build social rented units but their numbers will be as nothing compared with the mega-scale social housing that the Netherlands was famous for in the twentieth century. This sees our country getting in step with other Western European countries which, pressurized by globalization and EU guidelines, are engaged in slimming down their welfare states.

With the European welfare states shrinking and Europe adapting to the dictates of globalization, some architectural historians have seen fit to announce the end of social architecture in Europe. More than in the rest of the world, the architecture of twentieth-century Europe had a public, social character, as the architectural historian Hans Ibelings, for one, contended in 2011 in his *European Architecture Since 1890.* After the Industrial Revolution architecture became a public task and such buildings as schools, hospitals, libraries, theatres and, in the Netherlands, social housing units were built at the behest of government agencies and public or semi-public institutions. But population decline, economic downturn, globalization and the neoliberal belief that the market can do it all better than the government have meant not only less architecture being built in Europe but also the loss of its public character.

A year later the French architectural historian Jean-Louis Cohen came to the same conclusion in his epic postmodernist account *The Future of Architecture: Since 1889.* Since the outbreak of the financial crisis the big

European practices, such as those of Norman Foster and Rem Koolhaas, have landed most of their commissions in Russia, China and other state capitalist countries with questionable regimes. There, Cohen concludes in the postscript, they are realizing with increasing regularity the spectacle architecture that make the biggest waves on architecture sites and in the glossies. This way, architecture is steadily being reduced to making 'icons' with which the rich and powerful can cut a dash on the international stage.

At the same time, Cohen observes, the number of buildings being designed by architects, in Europe as well, is shrinking. He concludes his history on a sombre note: 'What still deserves to be called "architecture" would seem to amount to little more than a handful of diamonds amid the rubble of the planet. From this perspective, the socially engaged experiences of the twentieth century may prove to have been just a brief interlude in history's ongoing drama.'

But even though the future of architecture in Europe and the Netherlands looks grim, it doesn't mean that postmodernism is on the way out – quite the reverse, in fact. In *Shifts*, an essay Hans Ibelings co-authored in 2012 with the Powerhouse practice about the fundamental changes in European architecture at the start of the twenty-first century, Ibelings admits that he got it wrong 15 years ago when he pronounced postmodernism dead in his book *Supermodernism.* Nor is it just architecture where postmodernism is more alive than ever, but 'from literature to fact-free politics: the cultural relativism of "anything goes"' reigns everywhere. Contrary to his expectations at the end of the 1990s the digital age, powered by the internet, has strengthened postmodernism instead of eradicating it: 'Everything can go in any direction at all, can exist side by side.'

With this observation Ibelings was concurring with the makers of the major exhibition on postmodernism held at the Victoria and Albert Museum in London at the beginning of 2012. In many respects, the catalogue informs us, the quotes and the cut-and-past tactics that typified early postmodernist art and architecture 30 years ago were a harbinger of today's digital copy and paste. Now that the digital age is 20 years old, it proves to be in perfect keeping with the essence of postmodernism; the internet is pre-eminently the place where hierarchy is non-existent and everything co-exists on equal footing. There is no longer even a distinction between present and past, Ibelings and Powerhouse point out: the internet has no history. Posted messages are news for eternity and old pop songs are as easily obtainable as new ones and in exactly the same form – a digital file. There, past and present melt together into a permanent now, just as they are doing in architecture.

This eternal present, according to Ibelings, could also be said to signify an across-the-board stagnation in Western architecture and culture. The same starchitects who designed icons 20 years ago – Herzog & de Meuron, Zaha Hadid, Frank Gehry and in the Netherlands MVRDV – are still designing icons today.

This is of course an inevitable conclusion for those who have only now discovered that the digital age has not ushered in the end of postmodernism but strengthened it instead. Today's postmodernism, after all, is essentially no different to the postmodernism of thirty years ago. It is more of the same: wholesale fragmentation and 'things that exist side by side'. But just as history didn't end with the fall of the Wall in 1989, the development of architecture hasn't ended now. It may be more varied than ever stylistically, here as well these days, but it is still open to change.

During the past 20 years, postmodernism has grown into superpostmodernism. Dutch architects are enjoying an ever greater freedom. For example, the new decorativeness that accompanied the breakthrough of postmodernism in the Netherlands is becoming increasingly exuberant. Even figurative decorations have been back in favour in recent years.

Now that the crisis in building and architecture has entered its sixth year, there are changes afoot in Dutch architecture, major ones at that. The most important of these is that the machine driving the Dutch building industry – an aggregate of building enterprises and government assembled in the years after the Second World War to tackle the reconstruction – has ground to a halt. And as has become clear in the past few years, that machine will never again work as well as it did in the second half of the twentieth century. The age of mass housing construction, which went on to figure so prominently in the golden quarter century of Dutch architecture, has passed: the Vinex settlements were the last major government-driven housing developments to be built.

In view of the above, it doesn't require a crystal ball to predict that in the near future Dutch architecture will be more about small-scale briefs. Private patronage will have a greater say in the industry, not least in housing construction. And the reuse, restoration and renovation of existing buildings will become increasingly important.

Architecturally speaking then – and by way of conclusion – we can say that in these early years of the twenty-first century the Netherlands has become a mainstream Western European country.

De Stoep Theatre

Spijkenisse

UNStudio 2014

There is nowhere better to see Double Dutch in action than in Spijkenisse. In its restructured centre, SuperDutch and neo-traditionalist buildings amicably rub shoulders.

In the years 2009–2014 this Rotterdam satellite town renovated its centre along neo-traditionalist lines. Ashok Bhalotra, the father of all Vinex settlements, masterplanned the area and the post-modernist Sjoerd Soeters blocked it in. But Spijkenisse entrusted the cultural buildings on the rim of the new centre to two SuperDutch practices. MVRDV designed the library, Book Mountain, and Ben van Berkel's UNStudio Theatre de Stoep, a rippling white building that lights up oddly at night thanks to the dozens of spotlights in its roof.

About the authors

Bernard Hulsman (b. 1958) studied political science. The publications he has written for include *Ruslandbulletin*, *De Groene Amsterdammer*, *Vrij Nederland*, *Bouw*, *Archis*, *Forum*, *Kunstschrift* and *Museumtijdschrift*. Since 1990 Hulsman has been an editor of *NRC Handelsblad*, for which he writes articles on architecture, urban design and pop music, amongst other subjects.
He collaborated with fellow journalist Pieter Steinz on two books, *Reis om de wereld in tachtig hits* (Around the world in eighty hits, 2002) and *Zwanenzangen. De laatste liederen van vroeggestorven pophelden* (Swansongs: The last songs of pop heroes who died young, 2006). Hulsman has written a school book on architecture for teenagers, *Mijn gebouw wordt zo. Architectuur voor jongeren* (1999). In 2006 he published a book about fashions in architecture (*De krul en andere modes in de architectuur*) and in 2013 a book about row houses (*Het rijtjeshuis. De geschiedenis van een oer-Hollands fenomeen*), with photographs by Luuk Kramer. From 2002 to 2013 Hulsman taught at the Amsterdam Academy of Architecture.

Luuk Kramer (b. 1958) is a professional photographer who has worked for Claus en Kaan, Quist Wintermans, cepezed, Dam & Partners, Kraaijvanger and other architectural practices. Other clients include the Van Gogh Museum and Cruz y Ortiz for their renovation of the Rijksmuseum. His work has been published in books and professional magazines in the Netherlands and abroad. He has had one-man shows at the Hermitage (2009) and ARCAM (2011), both in Amsterdam. In the book *Nieuw Nieuw-West* (2010) his photographs provide a visual commentary on the urban restructuring of Amsterdam's Western Garden Suburbs (Westelijke Tuinsteden). He has worked with Bernard Hulsman on several books including *Heavens in Holland. Dutch Domes* (2010). A book about Dutch bridges (*De Nederlandse brug*), with photographs by Kramer, was published in 2013.

Credits

Text
Bernard Hulsman
Text editing
Mehgan Bakhuizen
Translation
John Kirkpatrick
Photography
Luuk Kramer
Photo p. 75
Rob 't Hart
Design
Joseph Plateau, Amsterdam
Printing
DeckersSnoeck, Gent, Belgium
Publisher
Eelco van Welie, nai010 publishers, Rotterdam

Front cover
Market Hall Rotterdam, MVRDV 2014
Back cover
Inverdan Zaandam, Soeters Van Eldonk architecten, 2013

www.nai010.com

nai010 publishers is an internationally oriented publisher specialized in developing, producing and distributing books on architecture, visual arts and related disciplines. www.nai010.com

ISBN 978-94-6208-160-4
Printed and bound in Belgium